AA Essen

Japanese
phrase book

AA Publishing

Contents

Introduction

● Welcome to the AA's new Essential Phrase Books series, covering the world's most popular languages and containing everything you'd expect from a comprehensive language series. They're concise, accessible and easy to understand, and you'll find them indispensable on your trip abroad.

Each guide is divided into 15 themed sections and starts with a pronunciation table which explains the phonetic pronunciation to all the words and phrases you'll need to know for your trip, while at the back of the book is an extensive word list and grammar guide which will help you construct basic sentences in your chosen language.

Throughout the book you'll come across coloured boxes with a 🖐 beside them. These are designed to help you if you can't understand what your listener is saying to you. Hand the book over to them and encourage them to point to the appropriate answer to the question you are asking.

Other coloured boxes in the book – this time without the symbol – give alphabetical listings of themed words with their English translations beside them.

For extra clarity, we have put all English words and phrases in black, foreign language terms in red and their phonetic pronunciation in italic.

This phrase book covers all subjects you are likely to come across during the course of your visit, from reserving a room for the night to ordering food and drink at a restaurant and what to do if your car breaks down or you lose your traveller's cheques and money. With over 2,000 commonly used words and essential phrases at your fingertips you can rest assured that you will be able to get by in all situations, so let the Essential Phrase Book become your passport to a secure and enjoyable trip!

Pronunciation table

Japanese is very easy to pronounce. It is made up of strings of syllables (a, ka, ta, etc.) which just join together following very simple rules of pronunciation (e.g. anata is *a-na-ta*). Unlike English, each syllable has mostly even stress and combinations of vowels (e-i, a-i, etc.) do not represent completely new sounds.

Vowels

Japanese has five vowels, pronounced either long or short. Distinguishing the length is very important as sometimes the meaning depends on the difference (e.g. ojisan/ojiisan, terms of address to a middle-aged man and an old man respectively). Note that a final e is always pronounced (e.g. sake, rice wine, is pronounced close to *sakay*).

a	like **a** in America	a	**asa**	*asa*
ā	ah (as in the exclamation !)	ah	**mā**	*mah*
e	**e** as in **pet** or	e	**desu**	*des*
	ay is in **sway**, but shorter	ay	**sake**	*sakay*
ē	**eh** sounded long, like **ere** in **there**	eh	**eetone**	*eh-to-nay*
i	like **i** in **pit**, though slightly longer	i	**nichi**	*nichi*
ī	**ee** as in **keep**	ee	**iie**	*ee-ye*
o	**o** as in **top**	o	**yoru**	*yoru*
ō	**ou** as in **four**	oh	**kyō**	*kyoh*
u	**u** as in **put**	u	**haru**	*haru*
ū	**oo** as in **coop**	oo	**chūmon**	*choomon*

Consonants

Most consonants are pronounced in a similar manner to English.

b	**b** as in **bat**	b	**bin**	*bin*
ch	**ch** as in **chip**	ch	**nichi**	*nichi*
d	**d** as in **day**	d	**dame**	*damay*
f	**f** as in **food**	f	**fuyu**	*fu-yu*
g	**g** as in **give**	g	**gogo**	*gogo*
h	**h** as in **hat**	h	**haru**	*haru*
j	**j** as in **jump**	j	**niji**	*niji*
k	**k** as in **king**	k	**koko**	*koko*
m	**m** as in **mat**	m	**totemo**	*totemo*
n	**n** as in **nut**.	n	**namae**	*nama-e*
	at the end of a word			
	may be more like **ng**	n (g)	**yen**	*yen (g)*
	ng as in **thing**	ng	**ringo**	*ring-o*
p	**p** as in **pat**	p	**posuto**	*pos-to*
r	Somewhere between English **r**,	r	**raigetsu**	*righ-gets*
	l and **d**. Never rolled **r**;			
	more like **r** in **car**			
s	**s** as in **start**	s	**semete**	*semetay*
sh	**sh** as in **ship**	sh	**shio**	*shi-o*
t	**t** as in **tip**	t	**dōshite**	*doh-shtay*
ts	**ts** as in **hits**	ts	**itsu**	*its*
w	**w** as in **watt**	w	**wakaru**	*wakaru*
y	**y** as in **yes**	y	**yoru**	*yoru*
z	**z** as in **zoo**	z	**mizu**	*mizu*

Note: when **i** and **u** follow **k**, **s**, **t**, **h**, **p** or come between two of them, they become very shortened and are often not heard at all (e.g. **desu** becomes *des* and **mimashita** becomes *mimashta*).

Vowel combinations

Basically, each vowel should be pronounced separately. The most common combinations are:

ai	**igh** as in h**igh**	**igh**	**hai**	*high*
ao	**ow** as in n**ow**	**ow**	**nao**	*now*
ei	**ay** as in pl**ay**	**ay**	**rei**	*ray*
ue	**weigh** as in w**eigh**t	**eigh**	**ue**	*weigh*

English edition prepared by First Edition Translations Ltd, Great Britain

Designed and produced by AA Publishing

Distributed in the United Kingdom by AA Publishing, Norfolk House, Priestley Road, Basingstoke, Hampshire RG24 9NY

First published in 1995 as Wat & Hoe Japans/© Uitgeverij Kosmos bv – Utrecht/Antwerpen

Van Dale Lexicografie bv – Utrecht/Antwerpen

This edition © The Automobile Association 1999

A CIP catalogue record for this book is available from the British Library

ISBN: 0 7495 2140 6

Published by AA Publishing (a trading name of Automobile Association Developments Limited, whose registered office is Norfolk House, Priestley Road, Basingstoke, Hampshire RG24 9NY. Registered number 1878835).

Typeset by Anton Graphics Ltd, Andover, Hampshire.

Printed and bound by S.T.I.G.E., Turin, Italy.

Cover photograph: beach at Hagi, AA Photo Library (D. Corrance)

Find out more about AA Publishing and the wide range of services the AA provides by visiting our web site at www.theaa.co.uk

Useful lists

1.1 Today or tomorrow?

What day is it today?	今日は何曜日ですか。
	kyoh-wa nan-yohbi des-ka
Today's Monday	今日は月曜日です。
	kyoh-wa gets-yohbi des
– Tuesday	今日は火曜日です。
	kyoh-wa ka-yohbi des
– Wednesday	今日は水曜日です。
	kyoh-wa swee-yohbi des
– Thursday	今日は木曜日です。
	kyoh-wa moku-yohbi des
– Friday	今日は金曜日です。
	kyoh-wa kin-yohbi des
– Saturday	今日は土曜日です。
	kyoh-wa do-yohbi des
– Sunday	今日は日曜日です。
	kyoh-wa nichi-yohbi des
in January	一月に
	ichi-gatsu-ni
since February	二月から
	ni-gatsu-kara
in spring	春に
	haru-ni
in summer	夏に
	natsu-ni
in autumn	秋に
	aki-ni
in winter	冬に
	fuyu-ni
1998	1998年
	sen-kyoo-hyaku-kyoo-joo-hachi-nen
the twentieth century	20世紀
	nijoo-say-ki
What's the date today?	今日は何日ですか。
	kyoh-wa nan-nichi des-ka
Today's the 24th	今日は24日です。
	kyoh-wa nijoo-yokka des
Monday 3 November 1998	1998年11月3日の月曜日
	sen-kyoo-hyaku-kyoo-joo-hachi-nen joo-ichi-gatsu mikka no gets-yohbi
in the morning	朝に
	asa-ni
in the afternoon	午後に
	gogo-ni
in the evening	夕方に
	yoogata-ni
at night	夜に
	yoru-ni
this morning	今朝
	kesa
this afternoon	今日の午後
	kyoh no gogo

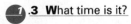
this evening _____	今日の夕方
	kyoh no yoogata
tonight _____	今晩
	kom-ban
last night _____	昨晩
	saku-ban
this week _____	今週
	kon-shoo
next month _____	来月
	righ-gets
last year _____	去年
	kyo-nen
next... _____	次の
	tsugi-no
in...days/weeks/ _____	…日／週間／か月／年間に
months/years	*... nichi/shookan/ka-getsu/nenkan-ni*
...weeks ago _____	…週間前に
	... shookan ma-e-ni
day off _____	休日
	kyoo-jitsu

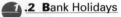 .2 Bank Holidays

New Year's Day (January 1)	gan-jitsu
Adult's Day (January 15)	sayjin-no-hi
National Foundation Day (February 11)	ken-koku ki-nen-bi
Vernal Equinox Day (March 21)	shun-bun-no-hi
Greenery Day (April 29)	midori-no-hi
Constitution Day (May 3)	kempoh ki-nen-bi
Public Holiday (May 4)	kokumin-no-kyoo-jitsu
Children's Day (May 5)	kodomo-no-hi
Marine Day (July 20)	umi-no-hi
Respect for the Aged Day (September 15)	kayroh-no-hi
Autumnal Equinox Day (September 23)	shoobun-no-hi
Health-Sports Day (October 10)	tigh-iku-no-hi
Culture Day (November 3)	bunka-no-hi
Labour Thanksgiving Day (November 23)	kinroh-kansha-no-hi
Emperor's Birthday (December 23)	tennoh tanjoh-bi

Though officially only January 1 is a public holiday during the New Year period, most banks and businesses remain shut until at least January 3. The period between April 29 and May 5 is known as Golden Week.

The Obon festival, when families return to ancestral homes to venerate the returning spirits of their ancestors, is held in country districts around mid July and in Tokyo in mid August. It should also be noted that Christmas Day is a normal business day.

.3 What time is it?

What time is it? _____	何時ですか。
	nanji des-ka
It's nine o'clock _____	（午前）9時です。
	(gozen) ku-ji des
– five past ten _____	（午前）10時5分…
	(gozen) joo-ji go-fun...

– a quarter past eleven _____	（午前）11時15分… *(gozen) joo-ichi-ji joo-go-fun...*
– twenty past twelve_____	（午後）12時20分… *(gogo) joo-ni-ji ni-juppun...*
– half past one _____	（午後）1時半… *(gogo) ichi-ji han...*
– twenty-five to three _____	（午後）2時35分… *(gogo) ni-ji san-joo-go-fun...*
– a quarter to four _____	（午後）3時45分… *(gogo) san-ji yon-go-go-fun...*
– ten to five _____	（午後）4時50分… *(gogo) yo-ji go-juppun...*
– twelve noon_____	12時／正午… *joo-ni-ji/shoh-go...*
– midnight _____	夜中の12時… *yo-naka no joo-ni-ji...*
half an hour _____	三十分間 *san-juppun-kan*
What time? _____	何時？ *nanji*
What time can I come _____ round?	何時に来れば いいですか。 *nanji-ni kureba ee des-ka*
At... _____	…に *... ni*
After... _____	…過ぎに *... sugi-ni*
Before... _____	…前に *... ma-e-ni*
Between...and... _____	…と…の間に *... to ... no ai-da-ni...*
From...to... _____	…から…まで *... kara ... maday*
In...minutes _____	…分後に *... fun go-ni*
– an hour _____	1時間後に *... ichi-jikan go-ni*
– ...hours _____	…時間後に *... jikan go-ni*
– a quarter of an hour _____	15分後に *joo-go-fun go-ni*
– three quarters of _____ an hour	45分後に *yon-joo-go-fun go-ni*
early/late _____	早過ぎます／遅過ぎます。 *haya-sugi-mas/oso-sugi-mas*
on time_____	間に合って／…に間に合います。 *mani-attay/... ni mani-a-imas*

1.4 One, two, three...

Numbers are rarely used on their own, but join with 'counters'. The counter can be joined after any of the numbers in the list below. For example, the counter for books is satsu, so that 'one book' is /is-satsu/, 'two books' is /ni-satsu/, etc.

Some of the most common counters are:

時 *ji* (hour): ichi-ji (1 o'clock), ni-ji (2 o'clock)

時間 *jikan* (hours): ichi-jikan (1 hour), ni-jikan (two hours)

枚 mai (used for flat objects like sheets of paper): ichi-migh, ni-migh, etc.
円 yen (the Japanese currency): hyaku-en (100 yen), sen(g)-en (1000 yen)
台 dai (for machines like cars and bikes): ichi-digh, ni-digh, etc.
杯 hai (cups): koh-hee ni-high (two cups of coffee), o-cha go-high (five cups of tea)
本 hon (for cylindrical objects, like chopsticks, cigarettes, etc.): ip-pon, ni-hon, sàm-bon
人 nin (people): san-nin (three people), roku-nin (six people). The words for one and two people are different: hi-to-ri (one person) and fu-ta-ri (two people).

However you can avoid using counters for the numbers one to ten by employing the alternative Japanese numbering system. They are shown in brackets in the list. For example, *hambahga mits kuda-sigh* is "Two hamburgers, please."

0	ray/zero
1	ichi (hi-tots)
2	ni (fu-tats)
3	san (mits)
4	shi/yon (yots)
5	go (i-tsuts)
6	roku (muts)
7	shichi/nana (na-nats)
8	hachi (yats)
9	ku/kyoo (koko-nots)
10	joo/ju (toh)
11	joo-ichi
12	joo-ni
13	joo-san
14	joo-shi
15	joo-go
16	joo-roku
17	joo-shichi
18	joo-hachi
19	joo-ku
20	ni-joo
21	ni-joo-ichi
22	ni-joo-ni
30	san-joo
31	san-joo-ichi
32	san-joo-ni
40	yon-joo
50	go-joo
60	roku-joo
70	nana-joo
80	hachi-joo
90	kyoo-joo
100	hyaku
101	hyaku ichi
110	hyaku joo
120	hyaku ni-joo
200	ni-hyaku
300	sam-byaku
400	yon-hyaku

Useful lists

500	*go-hyaku*
600	*rop-pyaku*
700	*nana-hyaku*
800	*hap-pyaku*
900	*kyoo-hyaku*
1000	*sen/issen*
1100	*sen hyaku*
2000	*ni-sen*
3000	*san-zen*
8000	*has-sen*
10,000	*ichi-man*
20,000	*ni-man*
100,000	*joo-man*
a million	*hyaku-man*
one hundred million	*oku*

1st	第一
	dai-ichi
2nd	第二
	dai-ni
3rd	第三
	dai-san
once	一倍
	ichi-bigh
twice	二倍
	ni-bigh
triple	三倍
	sam-bigh
half	半分
	ham-bun
a quarter	四分の一
	yon-bun no ichi
a third	三分の一
	sam-bun no ichi
a couple, a few, some	いくつかの／二、三
	iku-tsu ka no/ ni, san
2 + 4 = 6	2プラス4は6
	ni puras yon wa roku
4 – 2 = 2	4マイナス2は2
	yon mighnas ni wa ni
2 x 4 = 8	2かける4は8
	ni kakeru yon wa hachi
4 ÷ 2 = 2	4割る2は2
	yon waru ni wa ni
odd/even	偶数の／奇数の
	goo-soo no/ ki-soo no
total	全部（で）
	zem-bu (de)
6 x 9	長さは9メートル幅は6メートルです。
	nagasa wa kyoo meh-toru haba wa roku meh-toru

Is the weather going_____ to be good/bad?	いい／悪い天気になりますか。 *ee/warui tenki-ni narimas-ka*
Is it going to get _____ colder/hotter?	寒く／暑くなりますか。 *samuku/atsuku narimas-ka*
What temperature is it ____ going to be?	気温は何度ぐらいでしょうか。 *kion-wa nando gurigh deshoh-ka*
Is it going to rain?_____	雨になりますか。 *ame-ni narimas-ka*
Is there going to be a ____ storm?	嵐になりますか。 *arashi-ni narimas-ka*
Is it going to snow? _____	雪になりますか。 *yuki-ni narimas-ka*
Is it going to freeze?_____	氷が張りますか。 *kohri-ga harimas-ka*
Is the thaw setting in? ____	氷が溶けるぐらいの暖かさですか。 *kohri-ga tokeru gurai no atata-kasa des-ka*
Is it going to be foggy? ___	霧が立ちますか。 *kiri-ga tachimas-ka*
Is there going to be a ____ thunderstorm?	雷雨になりますか。 *righ-u-ni narimas-ka*
The weather's changing ___	天気がくずれます。 *tenki-ga kuzuremas*
It's cooling down_____	涼しくなります。 *suzushiku-narimas*
What's the weather _____ going to be like today/ tomorrow?	今日／明日の天気予報はどうですか。 *kyoh/ashta no tenki yo-hoh wa doh des-ka*

薄ら寒い chilly	酷暑 heat wave	嵐 stormy
快晴 clear	暑い hot	日当りのよい sunny
曇／くもり cloudy	台風 typhoon	雷雨 thunderstorm
寒い cold	穏やか mild	雨天 wet
湿っぽい damp	蒸し暑い muggy	風 wind
(氷点下) …度 ...degrees (above/ below zero)	どんよりした overcast	かすかな／強い風 light/moderate/ strong wind
霧雨 drizzle	雨 rain	風のある windy
いい天気 fine	猛暑 scorching hot	霰 sleet
霧 fog	にわか雨 shower	梅雨 rainy season
霜 frost	雪 snow	暖かい warm
ひょう hail	はやて squalls	

1.6 **H**ere, there...

See also 5.1 Asking for directions

here/there	ここ…そこ…あそこ
	koko/soko/a-soko
somewhere	どこか
	doko-ka
nowhere	どこにも…ない
	doko ni mo...nai
everywhere	どこにでも
	doko ni demo
far away/nearby	遠い…近い
	toh-i/chi-kigh
right/left	右の方に…左の方に
	migi no hoh ni/hidari no hoh ni
to the right/left of	…の右に／…の左に
	... no migi ni/... no hidari ni
straight ahead	真っ直ぐ
	mas-sugu
via	…経由で
	... kay-yu de
in	…の中に
	... no naka ni
on	…の上に
	... no u-e ni
under	…の下に
	... no shta ni
against	…に対して
	... ni tigh-shtay
opposite	…の向こう側に
	... no mukoh-gawa ni
next to	…の隣に
	... no tonari ni
near	…の側に
	... no soba ni
in front of	…の前に
	... no ma-e ni
in the centre	…の真ん中に
	... no man-naka ni
forward	前へ
	ma-e ay
down	下へ
	shta ay
up	上へ
	u-e ay
inside	中へ
	naka ay
outside	外へ
	soto ay
behind	後へ
	ushiro ay
at the front	前に
	ma-e ni
at the back	後に
	ushiro ni

in the north	北の方に	kita no hoh ni
to the south	南の方へ	minami no hoh ni
from the west	西の方から	nishi no hoh kara
from the east	東の方から	hi-gashi no hoh kara

1.7 What does that sign say?

危険
danger

注意
warning

応急手当
first aid

緊急ブレーキ／非常
ブレーキ
emergency brake

避難階段
fire escape

緊急出口／非常口
emergency exit

通行禁止
no thoroughfare

入場無料
no charge

禁煙
no smoking

喫煙
smoking

手をふれないで
ください。
please do not touch

ペンキ塗りたて
wet paint

芝生に入らないで
下さい。
keep off the grass

撮影禁止
no photographs

起こさないで
ください。
do not disturb

入口
entrance

出口
exit

案内
information

観光案内所
tourist information

受付け
reception

満員
full

営業中
open

準備中
closed

押／引
push/pull

故障中
out of order

予約済
reserved

支払い所
pay here

売出し
sale/clearance

売り物
for sale

階段
stairs

エスカレーター
escalator

エレベーター
lift

階
...floor

トイレ／お手洗い／
便所（女性／男性）
toilets/gents/
gentlemen/ladies

銀行
bank

警察署
police station

窓口
counter

切符
tickets

待合室
waiting room

停留所／バス停
bus stop

停車場／タクシー
乗り場
taxi stand

郵便箱／ポスト
post box

〒
mail

猛犬注意
beware of the dog

火気厳禁
no open fires

高圧注意
high voltage

足下注意
mind the step

立入禁止
no entry

ペット禁止
no pets allowed

営業時間
opening hours

私有地
private (property)

Useful lists

🕖 .8 Personal details

In Japan the family name comes first and the given name next. Titles come after the name. The title -*san* can be attached either to the surname or the given name, and is used for both males and females, being the equivalent of Mr, Mrs and Miss. Small children are addressed by their given name plus -*chan*, and boys by either their given name (among friends) or their surname (at school, for example) plus -*kun*. Superiors may also address subordinates in companies by their surname plus -*kun*. Anyone regarded as an intellectual is called *sensei* (sen-say, 'teacher').

your name_____	お名前
	onama-e
my name _____	名前
	nama-e
surname_____	名字（苗字）／姓
	myohji/say
given name(s)_____	名前
	nama-e
address_____	住所
	joo-sho
post code _____	郵便番号
	yoobin bango
sex (male/female) _____	性（男／女）
	say (dan/jo)
nationality _____	国籍
	koku-seki
date of birth _____	生年月日
	say-nen-gappi
place of birth _____	出生地
	shushoh-chi
occupation_____	職業
	shoku-gyoh
married/single/divorced____	既婚／未婚／離婚
	ki-kon/mi-kon/ri-kon
(number of) children _____	子供（の数）
	ko-domo (no kazu)
passport/identity card/_____	パスポート（旅券）／身分証明書／
driving licence number	運転免許書の番号
	pasu-pohto (ryo-ken)/mibun shoh-may-sho/
	unten men-kyo-sho no bango

Courtesies

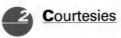

2 **C**ourtesies

The use of courtesies is considered important in Japan. When
someone does something for you, a simple *dohmo sumimasen* (thank
you for your trouble) is greatly appreciated. On meeting, the Japanese
greet each other with a bow from the waist, of varying depth. Non-
Japanese need not do so, though this is a custom which people find
themselves following almost unconsciously after a short time. Men in
particular may greet a European with a handshake. It is of utmost
importance that shoes are taken off when entering private homes.
There is a greater tolerance of proximity in Japan than in the U.K.; in
trains, lifts and other crowded public places, physical contact is
unavoidable. It is polite, however, to maintain a kind of mental privacy.
Impatience is rarely shown in public, while displays of anger cause
embarrassment and are rarely effective.

2 **.1 G**reetings

Good morning _____ おはよう（ございます）。
o-high-yoh (goza-i-masu)

Hello _____ こんにちは。
kon-nichi wa

Good evening_____ 今晩は。
kom-ban wa

Good afternoon _____ 今日は。
kon-nichi wa

How are you? _____ お元気ですか。
o-genki des-ka

Fine, thank you, and you?__ はい、元気です。あなたは？
high, genki des. anata wa

Very well _____ おかげさまで。
o-kagay-sama day

Not too bad_____ まあまあです。
mah mah des

I'd better be going_____ じゃあ、失礼します。
jah, shi-tsu-ray shimas

I have to be going. _____ 人を待たせていますので、
  Someone's waiting for me これで失礼いたします。
shto-o matasetay imas no day,
koray-de shi-tsu-ray itashimas

Goodbye _____ さよなら。
sayoh-nara

See you soon _____ またあとで。
mata ato-day

Good night _____ お休みなさい。
oyasumi nasa-i

Good evening_____ 今晩は。
kom-ban wa

Good luck _____ がんばって下さい。
gambattay kuda-sigh

Have fun_____ 楽しんで下さい。
tano-shinday kuda-sigh

Look after yourself _____ ごきげんよう！
gokigen-yoh

Have a nice holiday _____ 楽しい休暇を。
tanoshee kyookay-o

Have a good trip _____	楽しい旅行を。
	tanoshee ryokoh-o
Thank you, you too_____	どうもありがとう。あなたも。
	dohmo arigatoh, anata-mo
Say hello to...for me_____	…によろしく。
	... ni yoroshku

2.2 How to ask a question

Who?_____	誰？
	daray
Who's that? _____	誰ですか。
	daray des-ka
What? _____	何？
	nani
What's there to _____ see here?	この近くで何か面白いことがありますか。
	kono chikaku day nani-ka omoshiroi koto-ga arimas-ka
What kind of hotel _____ is that?	どんなホテルですか。
	donna hoteru des-ka
Where?_____	どこ？
	doko
Where's the toilet? _____	トイレはどこにありますか。
	toiray-wa doko-ni arimas-ka
Where are you going? ____	どちらに行かれますか。
	dochira-ni ikaremas-ka
Where are you from? _____	どこから来ましたか。
	doko-kara kimashta-ka
How?_____	どう？
	doh
How far is that? _____	どのくらい遠いですか。
	dono kurigh toh-i des-ka
How long does that take? _	何時間かかりますか。
	nan-jikan kakarimas-ka
How long is the trip? _____	旅行はどのくらいかかりますか。
	ryokoh-wa dono kurigh kakarimas-ka
How much?_____	いくらですか。
	ikura des-ka
How many?_____	いくつですか。
	ikutsu des-ka
How much is this?_____	これはいくらですか。
	koray-wa ikura des-ka
What time is it? _____	今何時ですか。
	ima nanji des-ka
Which....? _____	どの…？
	dono...
Which? _____	どれ？
	doray...
Which glass is mine? _____	どのコップが私のですか。
	dono koppu-ga watashi-no des-ka
When? _____	いつ？
	itsu
When are you leaving? ____	いつ出ますか。
	itsu demas-ka
Why?_____	どうして／なぜ
	dohshtay / nazay

Courtesies

2

Could you help me, _____ please?	手伝って下さいませんか。
	tetsudattay kudasa-i-masen-ka
Could you point that_____ out to me?	教えて下さいませんか。
	oshietay kudasa-i-masen-ka
Could you come _____ with me, please?	連れていって下さいませんか。
	tsuretay ittay kudasa-i-masen-ka
Could you reserve some __ tickets for me, please?	予約していただけますか。
	yoyaku shitay itadakemas-ka
Do you know...? _____	…（を）知っていますか。
	... (o) shtte imas-ka
Do you know another _____ hotel, please?	他のホテルを紹介して下さい。
	hoka-no hoteru-o shohkaigh shtay kuda-sigh
Do you have a...?_____	…（が）ありますか。
	... (ga) arimas-ka
Do you have a _____ vegetarian dish, please?	ベジタリアン料理はありますか。
	bejitarian-ryohri-wa arimas-ka
I'd like... _____	…お願いします。
	... onega-i-shimas
I'd like a kilo of apples, ____ please	リンゴを一キロ下さい。
	ringo-o ikkiro kuda-sigh
Can I take this?_____	これを持って行ってもいいですか。
	kore-o mottay ittay-mo ee des-ka
Can I smoke here?_____	タバコを吸ってもいいですか。
	tabako-o suttay-mo ee des-ka
Could I ask you _____ something?	すみませんが
	sumimasen-nga

2 .3 How to reply

Yes, of course_____	はい、もちろん。
	high, mochiron
No, I'm sorry_____	いいえ、すみません。
	ee-ye, sumimasen
Yes, what can I do _____ for you?	はい、どうぞ。
	high, dohzo
Just a moment, please ____	ちょっと待って下さい。
	chotto mattay kudasa-i
No, I don't have _____ time now	すみませんが、時間がありません。
	sumimasen-nga, jikan-nga arimasen
No, that's impossible _____	不可能です。
	fukanoh des
I think so _____	そう思います。
	soh omo-imas
No, no-one _____	誰もいません。
	dare-mo imasen
No, nothing_____	何もありません。
	nani-mo arimasen
That's right _____	それで結構です。
	soray-day kekkoh des
That's different_____	違います。
	chiga-i-masu
I agree_____	賛成です。
	sansay des
I don't agree _____	賛成出来ません。
	sansay dekimasen
All right _____	いいです。
	ee des

Okay	いいですよ
	ee des-yo
Perhaps	多分
	tabun
I don't know	わかりません／知りません
	wakarimasen/shirimasen

2 .4 Thank you

Thank you	（どうも）ありがとう。
	(dohmo) arigatoh
You're welcome	どういたしまして。
	doh itashi-mashtay
Thank you very much	どうもありがとうございます。
	dohmo arigatoh goza-i-mas
Very kind of you	ご親切に！
	go-shinsetsu-ni
I enjoyed it very much	本当に楽しかったです。
	hontoh-ni tanoshikatta des
Thank you for your trouble	どうもありがとうございました
	dohmo arigatoh goza-i-mashta
You shouldn't have	すみませんでした。
	sumimasen deshta
That's all right	どういたしまして。
	doh itashimashtay

2 .5 Sorry

Excuse me	すみません
	sumimasen
I'm sorry, I didn't know...	…知らなかったので、申し訳ありません。
	... shiranakatta no-day, mohshi-wakay-arimasen
I do apologise	すみませんでした。
	sumimasen deshta
I'm sorry	申し訳ありません。
	mohshi-wakay-arimasen
I didn't do it on purpose, it was an accident	わざとやったわけではないので、お許し下さい。
	waza-to yatta wakay de-wa-nai no-day, oyurushi-kuda-sigh
That's all right	いいですよ
	ee des-yo
Never mind	まあまあ
	mah mah
It could've happened to anyone	それは誰にでも起こりえることです。
	soray-wa daray-ni demo okori-eru koto des

2 .6 What do you think?

Which do you prefer?	どちらがお好きですか。
	dochira-ga o-ski des-ka
What do you think?	どう思いますか。
	doh omoimas-ka
Don't you like dancing?	踊るのが嫌いですか。
	odoru no-ga ki-righ des-ka
I don't mind	何でもいいです。
	nandemo ee des

Well done! _____ よかった。
yokatta

Not bad! _____ それほど悪くない！
soray hodo waruku-nai

Great! _____ すばらしい！
subarashee

Wonderful food! _____ おいしい！
oi-shee

It's really nice here! _____ 楽しいですねえ！
tanoshee des-ne

How nice! _____ すてき！
steki

How pretty! _____ きれい！
kiray

How nice for you! _____ いいですね。
ee des-ne

I'm very happy with... _____ …に満足しています。
... ni manzoku shitay imas

I'm not very happy _____ …に満足していません。
with...
... ni manzoku shitay imasen

I'm glad... _____ …うれしい。
... ureshee

I'm having a great time ___ とても楽しんでいます。
totemo tanoshinde imas

I'm looking forward to it ___ それを楽しみに待っています。
soray-o tanoshimi-ni mattay-imas

That's great _____ すごい！
sugoi

What a pity! _____ 残念！
zannen

That's ridiculous! _____ ばかばかしい！
baka-baka-shee

What a load of rubbish! ___ ばからしい！
bakara-shee

I don't like... _____ …は嫌いです。
... wa ki-righ des

I'm bored to death _____ うんざりだよ。
unzari da-yo

I've had enough _____ もうあきた。
moh akita

This is no good _____ だめ（だ）よ。
damay (da) yo

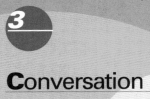

Conversation

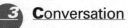
3 Conversation

3.1 I beg your pardon?

I don't speak any _____	ぜんぜん話せません。
	zen-zen ha-nase-masen
I speak a little... _____	少しだけ…話せます。
	skoshi dakay ... ha-nasay-mas
I'm English _____	私はイギリス人です。
	Watashi-wa igirisu-jin des
I'm Scottish _____	私はスコットランド人です。
	Watashi-wa sukottorando-jin des
I'm Irish _____	私はアイルランド人です。
	Watashi-wa irugh-rand-jin des
I'm Welsh _____	私はウェールズ人です。
	Watashi-wa wehruzu-jin des
Do you speak English/ French/German?	英語（フランス語／ドイツ語）は話せますか。
	Aygo/furansugo/doytsugo-wa hanasay-mas-ka
Is there anyone who speaks...?	ここには…が話せる人がいますか。
	koko ni-wa ... ga hanaseru shto-ga imas-ka
I beg your pardon?	何とおっしゃいましたか。
	nan-to ossha-i-mashta-ka
I understand	分かりました。
	wakarimashta
I don't understand	ちょっと分かりませんが。
	chotto wakarimasen-nga
Do you understand me?	分かりますか。
	wakarimas-ka
Could you repeat that, please?	もう一度言って下さい。
	moh ichido ittay kuda-sigh
Could you speak more slowly, please?	ゆっくり話して下さいませんか。
	yukkuri hanashtay kudasai-masen-ka
What does that mean?	それはどういう意味ですか。
	soray-wa doh yoo imi des-ka
What does that word mean?	その言葉はどういう意味ですか。
	sono kotoba-wa doh yoo imi des-ka
Is that similar to/ the same as...?	それは…という意味ですか。
	soray-wa... to yoo imi des-ka
Could you write that down for me, please?	それを書いて下さいませんか。
	soray-o kaitay kudasa-i-masen-ka
Could you point that out in this phrase book, please?	この本の中でそれを指さして下さいませんか。
	kono hon-no naka-de sore-o yubi-sashtay kudasa-i-masen-ka
One moment, please, I have to look it up	ちょっと待って下さい、捜してみます。
	chotto mattay kudasa-i, sagashtay mimas
I can't find the word	言葉が見つかりません。
	kotoba-ga mitsukarimasen
How do you say that in Japanese?	それは日本語でどう言いますか。
	soray-wa nihongo-de doh ee-mas-ka
How do you pronounce that?	それはどう発音しますか。
	soray-wa doh hatsuon shimas-ka

May I introduce myself? ___	自己紹介してもよろしいですか。
	jiko shohkigh shtay-mo yoroshee des-ka
My name's... _____	私は…です。
	watashi-wa... des
What's your name?_____	お名前は？
	onama-e-wa
May I introduce...? _____	ちょっとご紹介します。…さんです。
	chotto go-shohkigh shimas, ... san des
This is my wife_____	これは妻です。
	kore-wa tsuma des
This is my daughter _____	これは娘です。
	kore-wa musumay des
This is my mother_____	これは母です。
	kore-wa haha des
This is my friend _____	これは友達です。
	kore-wa tomodachi des
This is my husband _____	これは夫です。
	kore-wa otto des
This is my son _____	これは息子です。
	kore-wa musko des
This is my father _____	これは父です。
	kore-wa chichi des
How do you do _____	初めまして。どうぞよろしく。
	hajime-mashtay, dohzo yoroshku
Pleased to meet you_____	お目にかかれて嬉しいです。
	omay-ni kakaretay ureshee des
Where are you from? _____	お国はどちらですか。
	okuni-wa dochira des-ka
I'm from England/ _____ Scotland/Ireland/Wales	イギリス／スコットランド／アイルランド／ウェールズです。
	Igirisu/Sukottorando/Irughrando/ Wehruzu des
What city do you live in?___	どこにお住まいですか。
	doko-ni osu-migh des-ka
In..._____	…に
	... ni
It's near... _____	それは…に近い所です。
	soray-wa ... ni chi-kigh tokoro des
Have you been here _____ long?	もうお長いのですか。
	moh onagai no des-ka
A few days _____	二三日です。
	ni san nichi des
How long are you _____ staying here?	どのぐらいここにおられますか。
	dono gurigh koko-ni oraremas-ka
We're leaving tomorrow ___	明日立ちます。
	ashta tachimas
We're probably leaving ___ in two weeks	二週間後に立つつもりです。
	nishookan-go ni tatsu tsumori des
Where are you staying?____	どこにお泊りですか。
	doko-ni otomari des-ka
In a hotel _____	ホテルに
	hoteru-ni
With friends _____	友達の所に
	tomodachi-no tokoro-ni
With relatives _____	親戚の所に
	shinseki-no tokoro-ni

3

Conversation

Are you here on your own?	一人で来られましたか。 *shtori-day koraremashta-ka*
Are you here with your family?	ご家族とここに来ましたか。 *gokazoku-to koko-ni kimashta-ka*
I'm on my own	一人です。 *shtori des*
I'm with my wife	妻と来ました。 *tsuma-to kimashta*
I'm with my husband	夫と来ました。 *otto-to kimashta*
I'm with my family	家族と来ました。 *kazoku-to kimashta*
I'm with a friend/friends	友達と来ました。 *tomodachi-to kimashta*
Are you married?	結婚していますか。 *kekkon shtay imas-ka*
Do you have a steady boyfriend/girlfriend?	恋人いるの *koi-bito iru-no*
(female) That's none of your business	関係ないでしょ！ *(f) kankay-na-i desho*
(male) That's none of your business	関係ないだろ！ *(m) kankay-na-i daroh*
I'm married	結婚しています。 *kekkon shtay imasu*
– single	一人者です。 *shtorimono des*
– separated/divorced	離婚しています。 *rikon shtay imas*
– a widow/widower	未亡人／やもめです。 *miboh-jin/yamomay des*
I live with someone	恋人と住んでいます。 *koibito-to sunday imas*
Do you have any children?	お子さんは？ *oko-san-wa*
Do you have any grandchildren?	お孫さんは？ *omago-san-wa*
How old are you?	失礼ですが、何歳ですか。 *shitsuray des-nga, nansigh des-ka*
How old is she?	女の子はいくつですか。 *onna-no-ko wa ikutsu des-ka*
How old is he?	男の子はいくつですか。 *otoko-no-ko wa ikutsu des-ka*
I'm...	…歳です。 *...sigh des*
She's/he's...	…歳です。 *...sigh des*
What do you do for a living?	お仕事は何ですか。 *oshigoto-wa nan des-ka*
I work in an office	会社で働いています。 *kighsha-de hata-right-tay imas*
I'm a student/ I'm at school	学生です。 *gaksay des*
I'm unemployed	無職です。 *mushoku des*
I'm retired	退職しました。 *tigh-shoku shimashta*

I'm on a disability pension	障害者です。 *shoh-gigh-sha des*
I'm a housewife	主婦です。 *shufu des*
Do you like your job?	お仕事は面白いですか。 *o-shigoto-wa omoshiroi des-ka*
Most of the time	たいがいは。 *tigh-gigh-wa*
I usually do, but I prefer holidays	まあまあですが、休みの方が面白いですよね。 *mah mah des-nga, yasumi-no hoh-nga* *omoshiroi des-yo-ne*

3 .3 Starting/ending a conversation

Excuse me	すみませんが *sumimasen-nga*
Excuse me, could you help me?	すみませんが、助けて下さい。 *sumimasen-nga, tasketay kuda-sigh*
Yes, what's the problem?	どうしましたか。 *doh shimashta-ka*
What can I do for you?	何かご用でしょうか。 *nani-ka goyoh deshoh-ka*
Sorry, I don't have time now	急ぎますので、すみません。 *isogimas noday, sumimasen*
Do you have a light?	火をおもちですか。 *hi-o mochi des-ka*
May I join you?	ご一緒させていただいてもよろしいですか。 *goissho sasete itadigh-tay-mo yoroshee des-ka*
Could you take a picture of me/us?	写真をとってくださいますか。 *shashin-o tottay kudasaimas-ka*
Press this button	このボタンを押して下さい。 *kono botan-o oshtay kuda-sigh*
(female) Leave me alone	ほっといてよ！ *hotto itay-yo*
(male) Leave me alone	ほっといてくれよ！ *hotto itay kuray-yo*
(female) Get lost	あっちいってよ！ *achi ittay-yo*
(male) Get lost	あっちいけよ！ *achi ikay-yo*
(female) Go away or I'll scream	行かないと叫ぶわよ！ *ikanai-to, sakebu-wa-yo*
(male) Go away or I'll yell	行かないと叫ぶよ！ *ikanai-to, sakebu-yo*

3 .4 Congratulations and condolences

Happy birthday/many happy returns	お誕生日おめでとうございます。 *otanjohbi omedetoh gozaimas*
Please accept my condolences	心からお悔やみ申し上げます。 *kokoro-kara o-kuyami mohshi-agemas*

3.5 A chat about the weather

See also 1.5 The weather

It's so hot today! _____	今日は暑いですね。
	kyoh-wa atsui des-ne
It's so cold toady! _____	今日は寒いですね。
	kyoh-wa samui des-ne
Nice weather, isn't it? _____	いい天気ですね。
	ee tenki des-ne
What a wind! _____	すごい風ですね。
	sugoi kazay des-ne
All that rain! _____	すごい雨ですね。
	sugoi amay des-ne
All that snow! _____	雪が凄いですね。
	yuki-wa sugoi des-ne
All that fog! _____	深い霧ですね。
	fukigh kiri des-ne
Has the weather been ____	この天気はもう長いんですか。
like this for long here?	*kono tenki-wa moh nagai-n des-ka*
Is it always this hot _____	この辺はいつも暑いんですか。
here?	*kono hen-wa itsumo atsui-n des-ka*
Is it always this cold _____	この辺はいつも寒いんですか。
here?	*kono hen-wa itsumo samui-n des-ka*
Is it always this dry here? _	この辺はいつも雨が少ないんですか。
	kono hen-wa itsumo amay-nga sukunai-n des-ka
Is it always this wet here?_	この辺はいつも雨が多いですか。
	kono hen-wa itsumo amay-nga oh-ee des-ka

3.6 Hobbies

Do you have any _____	趣味は？
hobbies?	*shoomi-wa*
I like knitting _____	編みものが好きです。
	amimono-ga ski des
I like reading _____	読書が好きです。
	dokusho-ga ski des
I like photography _____	写真をとるのが好きです。
	shashin-o toru-no-ga ski de
I like music _____	音楽が好きです。
	ongaku-ga ski des
I like playing the guitar ___	ギターを弾くのが好きです。
	gitah-o hiku-no-ga ski des
I like playing the piano ___	ピアノを弾くのが好きです。
	piano-o hiku-no-ga ski des
I like going to the _____	映画を見に行くのが好きです。
movies	*ayga-o mi-ni iku-no-ga ski des*
I like travelling _____	旅行するのが好きです。
	ryokoh suru-no-ga ski des
I like sport _____	スポーツが好きです。
	spohtsu-ga ski des
I like fishing_____	つりに行くのが好きです。
	tsuri-ni iku-no-ga ski des
I like walking_____	散歩するのが好きです。
	sampo suru-no-ga ski des

3.7 Being the host(ess)

See also 4 Eating out

Can I offer you a drink? ____	何かお飲みになりませんか。 *nani-ka onomi-ni-narimasen-ka*
What would you like to drink? ____	何をお飲みになりますか。 *nani-o onomi-ni narimas-ka*
Would you like a _____ cigarette?	タバコはいかがですか。 *tabako-wa ikaga des-ka*
Would you like a cigar? ____	葉巻はいかがですか。 *hamaki-wa ikaga des-ka*
Something non-alcoholic,____ please	アルコールなしの飲み物を下さい。 *arukohru-nashi no nomimono-o kuda-sigh*
I don't smoke ____	たばこは吸いません。 *tabako-wa suimasen*

3.8 Invitations

Are you doing anything ____ tonight?	もう今晩の予定は何か決めたの。 *moh komban-no yotay-wa nani-ka kimeta-no*
Do you have any plans ____ for today/this afternoon?	もう今日の計画は出来ましたか。 *moh kyoh-no kaykaku-wa dekimashta-ka*
Do you have any plans ____ for tonight?	もう今晩の計画は出来ましたか。 *moh komban-no kaykaku-wa dekimashta-ka*
Would you like to go ____ out with me?	一緒に出かけませんか。 *isshoh-ni dekakemasen-ka*
Would you like to go ____ dancing with me?	一緒にダンスに行きませんか。 *isshoh-ni dansu-ni ikimasen-ka*
Would you like to have ____ lunch/dinner with me?	一緒に食べませんか。 *isshoh-ni tabemasen-ka*
Would you like to come ____ to the beach with me?	一緒に海岸に行きませんか。 *isshoh-ni kighgan-ni ikimasen-ka*
Would you like to come ____ into town with us?	一緒に町へ行きませんか。 *isshoh-ni machi-e ikimasen-ka*
Would you like to come ____ and see some friends with us?	一緒に友達の所に行きませんか。 *isshoh-ni tomodachi-no tokoro-ni ikimasen-ka*
I don't dance ____	踊りません。 *odorimasen*
Shall we sit at the bar? ____	バーに座らない？ *bah-ni suwara-nigh?*
Shall we get something ____ to drink?	何か飲みましょうか。 *nani-ka nomi-mashoh-ka*
Shall we go for a walk? ____	散歩に行きましょうか。 *sampoh-ni iki-mashoh-ka*
Shall we go for a drive? ____	ドライブに行きましょうか。 *drighb-ni iki-mashoh-ka*
Yes, all right ____	いいね。 *ee-ne*
Good idea ____	いい考え *ee kangae*
No (thank you) ____	いいえ、けっこうです *ee-ye, kekkoh des*
Maybe later ____	多分今度。 *tabun kondo*

Conversation

3

(female) I don't feel like it	興味がないわ。 *kyohmi-nga nigh-wa*
(male) I don't feel like it	興味がないよ。 *kyohmi-nga nigh-yo*
(female) I don't have time	時間がないわ。 *jikan-nga nigh-wa*
(male) I don't have time	時間がないよ。 *jikan-nga nigh-yo*
I already have a date	もう他の約束が。 *moh hoka-no yakusoku-nga*
I'm not very good at dancing	ダンスは下手です。 *dans-wa heta-des*
I'm not very good at volleyball	バレーボールは下手です。 *baray-bohru-wa heta-des*
I can't swim	泳げません。 *oyogemasen*

3.9 Paying a compliment

You look wonderful!	おきれいですね。 *okiray des-ne*
I like your car!	いい車ですね！ *ee kuruma des-ne*
What a sweet child!	何てかわいい赤ちゃんでしょう。 *nantay kawa-ee akachan deshoh*
You're a wonderful dancer!	ダンスが上手ですね。 *dans-ga johzu des-ne*
You're a wonderful cook!	料理が上手ですね。 *ryohri-ga johzu des-ne*
You're a terrific tennis player!	テニスが上手ですね。 *tenisu-ga johzu des-ne*

3.10 Chatting someone up

I like being with you	一緒にいるのが楽しい。 *isshoh-ni iru-no-ga tanoshee*
(female) I've missed you so much	とっても寂しかったわ。 *tottemo sabishikatta-wa*
(male) I've missed you so much	とっても寂しかったよ。 *tottemo sabishikatta-yo*
(female) I dreamt about you	あなたを夢にみたわ。 *anata-o yumay-ni mita-wa*
(male) I dreamt about you	君を夢にみたよ。 *kimi-o yumay-ni mita-yo*
You're pretty!	きれいだよ。 *kiray da-yo*
(female) You're nice	すてきよ。 *steki-yo*
(male) You're nice	すてきだよ。 *steki da-yo*
You're sexy	セクシー。 *sekshee*
(female) Look at me	私を見て。 *watashi-o mitay*
(male) Look at me	僕を見て。 *boku-o mitay*

You have such beautiful ___ eyes	きれいな瞳だね。
	kiray-na shtomi da-ne
(female) I'm crazy about ___ you	あなたに夢中なの。
	anata-ni muchoo na no
(male) I'm crazy about ___ you	君に夢中なんだ。
	kimi-ni muchoo nanda
I love you_____	愛してる。
	igh-shteru
(female) I love you too____	私も。
	watashi-mo
(male) I love you too ____	僕も。
	boku-mo
(female) I don't feel as ___ strongly about you	私の気持ちは違うの。
	watashi-no kimochi-wa chigau-no
(male) I don't feel as _____ strongly about you	僕の気持ちは違うんだ。
	boku-no kimochi-wa chigaun-da
I already have a _____ boyfriend/girlfriend	もう恋人がいます。
	moh koibito-ga imas
I'm not ready for that_____	もう少し待って。
	moh skoshi mattay
(female) This is going ____ too fast for me	すごく早過ぎるの。
	sugoku haya-sugiru-no
(male) This is going _____ too fast for me	すごく早過ぎるよ。
	sugoku haya-sugiru-yo
(female) Take your hands _ off me	触らないで。
	sawara-nigh-day
Okay, no problem _____	いいよ。
	ee-yo
Will you stay with me ____ tonight?	今夜一緒に泊まらない？
	konya issoh-ni tomara-nigh?
I'd like to go to bed _____ with you	愛したい。
	igh-shtigh
Only if we use a condom _	コンドームを使ってくれるなら。
	kondom-o tsukattay kureru-nara
We have to be careful ____ about AIDS	エイズのこともあるからね。
	ayzu-no koto-mo aru kara-ne
(female) That's what they _ all say	男って皆そういうのね。
	otokot-tay mina soh yoo no-ne
(female) We shouldn't ____ take any risks	危険は避けましょうよ。
	kiken-wa sakay mashoh-yo
(male) We shouldn't _____ take any risks	危険は避けようよ。
	kiken-wa sakay-yoh-yo
Do you have a condom? ___	コンドームもってる？
	kondom motteru?
(female) No? In that case _ we won't do it	それなら、やめましょう。
	sore-nara, yamemashoh
(male) No? In that case ____ we won't do it	それなら、やめよう。
	sore-nara, yameyoh

3.11 Arrangements

When will I see _____ you again?	またいつ会える。 *mata itsu aeru*
Are you free over the ____ weekend?	この週末おひまですか。 *kono shoomatsu ohima des-ka*
What shall we arrange? ____	何か計画しましょうか。 *nani-ka kay-kaku shimashoh-ka*
Where shall we meet? ____	どこで会いましょうか。 *doko-de aimashoh-ka*
Will you pick me/us up? ___	車で拾ってくださいますか。 *kuruma-de hirottay kudasaimas-ka*
Shall I pick you up? _____	車で拾って上げましょうか。 *kuruma-de hirottay agemashoh-ka*
I have to be home by... ____	…時までに帰らなければなりません。 *...ji-made-ni kaera-nakeraba-narimasen*
(female) I don't want ____ to see you anymore	もう会いたくないわ。 *moh aitaku-nigh-wa*
(male) I don't want to ____ see you anymore	もう会いたくないよ。 *moh aitaku-nigh-yo*

3.12 Saying goodbye

Can I take you home? ____	送っていってもいいですか。 *okuttay ittay-mo ee des-ka*
Can I write? ____	手紙を書いてもいいですか。 *tegami-o kaitay-mo ee des-ka*
Can I call you? ____	電話をかけてもいいですか。 *denwa-o kaketay-mo ee des-ka*
Will you write to me? ____	手紙をくれますか。 *tegami-o kuremas-ka*
Will you call me? ____	電話をくれますか。 *denwa-o kuremas-ka*
Can I have your _____ address?	あなたの住所を教えてくれますか。 *anata-no joosho-o oshietay kuremas-ka*
Can I have your phone ____ number?	あなたの電話番号を教えてくれますか。 *anata-no denwa bango-o oshietay kuremas-ka*
Thanks for everything ____	いろいろありがとうございました。 *iro-iro arigatoh goza-i-mashta*
It was very nice _____	とても楽しかったです。 *totemo tanoshikatta des*
Say hello to... _____	…さんによろしく。 *... san ni yoroshku*
All the best _____	元気でね。 *genki de-ne*
When will you be back? ___	いつ帰る？ *itsu kaeru?*
(female) I'll be waiting ____ for you	待ってるわ。 *matteru-wa*
(male) I'll be waiting ____ for you	待ってるよ。 *matteru-yo*
(female) I'd like to see ____ you again	また会いたいわ。 *mata ai-tigh-wa*

(male) I'd like to see _____ you again	また会いたいなあ。 *mata ai-tigh-nah*
This is our address. If _____ you're ever in the UK, you'd be more than welcome	私たちの住所です。いつでもイギリスにいらしたらどうぞ。 *watashi-tachi-no joosho des. itsu-demo* *igirisu-ni irashtara dohzo*

Conversation

Eating out

4 Eating out

● **Large cities like Tokyo** offer a vast selection of restaurants with food from all over the world. American fast food chain outlets can be found in most neighbourhoods near railway stations. Very popular too are 'family restaurants', where wide-ranging menus offer budget-priced dishes to suit the whole family. All department stores have two or more restaurant floors, with individual restaurants serving most varieties of Japanese, Chinese and Western food. In addition there is usually a large customers' restaurant, again with a wide selection. Food selection is made very easy in Japan because all restaurants display in their window wax models of the dishes offered and their prices. Family restaurants provide a fully illustrated menu. Only very expensive, up-market restaurants do not do this. Children are almost always welcome at local restaurants and those in the popular shopping centres and stations. Traditional restaurants with *tatami* (straw-matted) floors are a boon for those with babies.

4 .1 On arrival

I'd like to book a table for seven o'clock, please	七時にテーブルを予約したいのですが。 *shichiji-ni tehburu-o yoyaku shi-tigh no des-nga*
I'd like a table for two, please	二人用のテーブルをお願いします。 *futari-yoh-no tehburu-o onegigh shimas*
We've booked	予約しました。 *yoyaku shimashta*
we haven't booked	予約していません。 *yoyaku shtay imasen*
What time does the restaurant open	レストランは何時からオープンですか。 *restoran-wa nanji-kara ohpen des-ka*
What time does the restaurant close?	レストランは何時までですか。 *restoran-wa nanji maday des-ka*
Can we wait for a table?	テーブルが空くまで待ちたいのですが。 *tehburu-ga aku-made machi-tigh no des-nga*
Do we have to wait long?	長く待ちますか。 *nagaku machimas-ka*
Is this seat taken?	この席、空いてますか。 *kono seki ightay imas-ka*
Could we sit here?	ここに座ってもいいですか。 *koko-ni suwatte-mo ee des-ka*
Could we sit there?	あそこに座ってもいいですか。 *asoko-ni suwatte-mo ee des-ka*
Can we sit by the window?	窓ぎわに座ってもいいですか。 *mado-giwa-ni suwatte-mo ee des-ka*

ご予約ですか	Do you have a reservation?
お名前は	What name, please?
こちらへ	This way, please
このテーブルは予約済みです。	This table is reserved
15分お待ちいただくと 　テーブルが空きます。	We'll have a table free in fifteen minutes.
（バーで） 　お待ちになりますか	Would you like to wait (at the bar)?

Can we eat outside? _____	外でも食べられますか。
	soto demo taberaremas-ka
Do you have another _____ chair for us?	椅子もう一個ありますか。
	isu moh ikko arimas-ka
Do you have a highchair? __	子供用の椅子がありますか。
	kodomo-yoh-no isu-ga arimas-ka
Could you warm up this ___ bottle/jar for me?	すみませんが、このびんを暖めてくれますか。
	sumimasen-ga, kono bin-o atatametay kure-mas-ka
Not too hot, please _____	熱過ぎないように。
	atsu-suginigh yoh-ni
Is there somewhere I _____ can change the baby's nappy?	ベビールームありますか。
	bebee-room arimas-ka
Where are the toilets? _____	トイレはどこですか。
	toireh-wa doko des-ka

4.2 Ordering

Waiter! _____	ウェーターさん
	wehtah-san!
Waitress! _____	ウェートレスさん
	wehtres-san!
We'd like something _____ to eat	何か食べたいんですが。
	nani-ka tabe-tigh-n des-nga
We'd like a drink _____	何か飲みたいんですが。
	nani-ka nomi-tigh-n des-nga
Could I have a quick _____ meal?	何か速く出来る品はありますか。
	nani-ka hayaku dekiru shina-wa arimas-ka
We don't have much _____ time	急いでいるのですが。
	isoiday iru no des-nga
We'd like to have a _____ drink first	先ず何か飲みたいんですが
	mazu nani-ka nomi-tig-n des-nga
Do you have a menu _____ in English?	英語のメニューはありますか。
	aygo no menyoo-wa arimas-ka
Do you have a dish _____ of the day?	今日のメニューはありますか。
	kyoh no menyoo-wa arimas-ka
We haven't made a _____ choice yet	まだ決りません。
	mada kimarimasen
What do you _____ recommend?	お薦め品は何ですか。
	o-susume-hin-wa nan des-ka
What are the specialities? __	特別料理は何ですか。
	tokubetsu ryohri nan des-ka
I don't like... _____	…は好きじゃないんです。
	... wa ski ja nigh-n des
I don' like fish _____	魚は好きじゃないんです。
	sakana-wa ski ja nigh-n des
I don't like meat _____	肉は好きじゃないんです。
	niku-wa ski ja nigh-n des
What's this? _____	これは何ですか。
	koray-wa nan des-ka
Does it have...in it? _____	…が入っていますか。
	... nga ha-ittay imas-ka
Is this a hot dish? _____	この料理は暖かいですか。
	kono ryohri-wa atatá-kigh des-ka
Is this a cold dish? _____	この料理は冷たいですか。
	kono ryohri-wa tsume-tigh des-ka

Is this sweet? _____	この料理は甘いですか。
	kono ryohri-wa a-migh des-ka
Is this spicy? _____	この料理はからいですか。
	kono ryohri-wa ka-righ des-ka
Do you have anything _____ else, please?	他に何かありますか。
	hoka-ni nani-ka arimas-ka
I'm on a salt-free diet _____	塩ぬきでお願いします。
	sheeo-nuki-de onegai-shimas
I can't eat pork _____	豚肉は食べられません。
	butaniku-wa taberare-masen
– sugar _____	砂糖は食べられません。
	satoh-wa taberare-masen
– fatty foods _____	油っぽい料理は食べられません。
	aburap-poy ryohri-wa taberare-masen
– (hot) spices _____	（辛い）スパイスは食べられません。
	(karigh) spighs-wa taberare-masen
I'll/we'll have what those people are having	あの人と同じ料理を、お願いします。
	ano-shto-to onaji ryohri-o onegai-shimas
I'd like... _____	…お願いします。
	... onegai-shimas
Do you have a knife _____ and fork?	ナイフとフォークありますか。
	nighf to fohk arimas-ka
A little more rice please ___	ご飯もう少しお願いします。
	gohan moh skoshi onegai-shimas
Another glass of water please	水もう一杯お願いします。
	mizu moh ip-pigh onegai-shimas
One more please_____	もう一つお願いします。
	moh hitotsu onegai-shimas
Do you have salt and _____ pepper?	塩と胡椒ありますか。
	sheeo to koshoh arimas-ka
Do you have a napkin? ____	ナプキンありますか。
	napukin arimas-ka
Do you have a spoon? _____	スプーンありますか。
	spoon arimas-ka
Do you have an ashtray? __	灰皿ありますか。
	high-zara arimas-ka
Do you have any _____ matches?	マッチありますか。
	match arimas-ka
Do you have any _____ toothpicks?	つまようじありますか。
	tsuma-yohji arimas-ka
Can I have a glass of _____ water please	水一杯お願いします。
	mizu ippigh onegai-shimas
Do you have a straw? _____	ストローありますか。
	stroh arimas-ka
Let's begin_____	いただきましょう。
	itadakimashoh
Cheers! _____	乾杯
	kam-pigh
The next round's on me ___	今度は私がおごります。
	kondo-wa watashi-nga ogorimas

Eating out

See also 8.2 Settling the bill

How much is this dish?	この料理はいくらですか。 *kono ryohri-wa ikura des-ka*
Could I have the bill, please?	お勘定、お願いします。 *okanjoh onegigh-shimas*
All together	全部で *zembu-de*
Everyone pays separately	各自が払いますので。 *kakuji-nga haraimas no-de*
Could we have the menu again, please?	もう一回メニューを見せて下さい。 *moh ik-kigh menyoo-o misetay kuda-sigh*
The...is not on the bill	…が入っていません。 *... ga hight-tay imasen*

4 .4 **C**omplaints

It's taking a very long time	ずいぶん長くかかっていますね。 *zuibun nagaku kakattay imas-ne*
We've been here an hour already	もう一時間も待っています。 *moh ichi-jikan-mo mattay imas*
This must be a mistake	これは間違いでしょう。 *koray-wa machigigh deshoh*
This is not what I ordered	これは注文しませんでした。 *koray-wa choomon shimasen deshta*
I ordered...	…を注文しました。 *... o choomon shimashta*
There's a dish missing	料理が一品不足です。 *ryohri-ga ippin fusoku des*
This is broken	これは壊れています。 *kore-wa kowarete-imas*
This is not clean	ちょっとこれきたないのですが。 *chotto koray kita-nigh no des-nga*
The food's cold	料理が冷たいんです。 *ryohri-ga tsume-tigh-n des*
– not fresh	これは新鮮じゃないです。 *koray-wa shinsen ja nigh des*
– too salty	これは塩辛いです。 *koray-wa sheeo ka-righ des*
– too sweet	これは甘過ぎます。 *koray-wa ama-sugimas*
– too spicy	これは辛過ぎます。 *koray-wa kara-sugimas*
The meat's not done	肉は焼き足りません。 *niku-wa yaki-tarimasen*
– overdone	肉は焼き過ぎです。 *niku-wa yaki-sugi des*
– tough	肉が堅いんです。 *niku-ga ka-tigh-n des*
– off	肉がくさっています。 *niku-ga kusattay imas*
Could I have something else instead of this?	代わりの品を下さいませんか。 *kawari-no shina-o kudasaimasen-ka*
The bill/this amount is not right	勘定が合いません。 *kanjoh-nga aimasen*

We didn't have this _____	これは食べませんでした。
	koray-wa tabe-masen deshta
There's no paper in _____ the toilet	トイレットペーパーがないんです。
	toiretto-pehpah-ga nigh-n des
Will you call the _____ manager, please?	責任者を呼んでください。
	sekinin-sha-o yonday kuda-sigh

4.5 Paying a compliment

That was a wonderful _____ meal	とてもおいしかったです。
	totemo oishikatta-des
The food was excellent _____	ごちそうさまでした。
	gochisoh sama deshta
The...in particular was _____ delicious	特に…がとてもおいしかったです。
	toku-ni ... nga totemo oishikatta-des

4.6 The menu

The following are some of the most popular Japanese dishes.

しゃぶしゃぶ　　Shabu shabu

Thin strips of pork or lamb and various vegetables cooked in front of you in boiling water and eaten in dipping sauces.

焼き鳥　　Yakitori

Marinated chicken pieces on skewers, cooked over a brazier.

味噌汁　　Misoshiru

Soup made from miso (paste of fermented soy beans) with tofu and vegetables such as cabbage and small mushrooms.

うどん、そば　　Udon, soba

Thick white and thin brown noodles respectively. Served either cold with dipping sauces (good in summer) or warm in a soup.

茶わんむし　　Chawan-mushi

Fish and vegetables steamed in an egg custard.

豚カツ　　Tonkatsu

Pork cutlets fried in breadcrumbs and served with a thick brown sauce.

親子どんぶり　　Oyako donburi

Chicken and egg served on rice. A popular lunch dish.

カレーライス　　Karee raisu (karay righ-su)

The Japanese version of curry and rice. Usually beef, chicken or pork pieces in a curry sauce.

On the road

5.1 **A**sking for directions

Excuse me, could I ask you something?	すみませんが *sumimasen-nga*
I've lost my way	道に迷ってしまったんですが。 *michi-ni mayottay shimattan-des-nga*
Is there a(n)... around here?	この辺に…がありますか。 *kono hen-ni ... ga arimas-ka*
Is this the way to...?	この道は…へ行きますか。 *kono michi-wa ... e ikimas-ka*
Could you tell me how to get to the... (name of place)by car/on foot?	…へどう行くか教えて下さいませんか。 *... e doh iku-ka oshietay kudasai-masen-ka*
What's the quickest way to...?	…への一番速い道はどう行きますか。 *... e no ichiban hayai michi-wa doh ikimas-ka*
How many kilometres is it to...?	…まで何キロぐらいですか。 *... maday nankiro-gurigh-n des-ka*
Could you point it out on the map?	この地図で指差して下さい。 *kono chizu-de yubi-sashtay kuda-sigh*
My children are entered on this passport	子供はこのパスポートに記入してあります。 *kodomo-wa kono pas-pohto-ni kinyoo shitay arimas*
I'm travelling through	通過していきます。 *tsooka shtay imas*

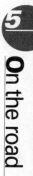

すみませんが、知りません。	I don't know, I don't know my way around here
道が違います。	You're going the wrong way
…に戻らなければなりません。	You have to go back to...
そこに着いたら、もう一度尋ねてください。	When you get there, ask again

真っ直ぐ straight ahead	信号 the traffic light	高架橋 the fly-over
左に left	トンネル the tunnel	橋 the bridge
右に right	一旦停止標識 the 'give way' sign	踏切 the level crossing/ the boom gates
渡って cross	建物／ビル the building	矢印 the arrow
交差点 the intersection	曲がり角で at the corner	
道 the street	川 the river	

A passport is necessary for all visitors to Japan. Citizens of most European countries do not need a visa if they are staying as tourists up to 90 days. Visitors from the US, Canada and New Zealand need a visa for visits of over 90 days. They are easily obtainable and free. Visitors from Australia need a visa for any visit. Drugs, firearms and pornography may not be taken into Japan. Non-residents can take in duty-free 400 cigarettes, or 100 cigars, or 500g of tobacco; 3 bottles of alcohol (760cc each); 50g perfume; and other goods up to 200,000 yen in value. Personal possessions are exempt.

パスポートを見せて下さい。＿＿＿＿＿	Your passport, please
ビザを見せて下さい。＿＿＿＿＿	Your visa, please
どこへ行きますか。＿＿＿＿＿	Where are you heading?
どのくらい滞在しますか。＿＿＿＿＿	How long are you planning to stay?
申告する品はありますか。＿＿＿＿＿	Do you have anything to declare?
これを開けて見せて下さい。＿＿＿＿＿	Open this, please

I'm going on holiday to... __	休暇で…へ行きます。 *kyooka-de ... e ikimas*
I'm on a business trip _____	出張です。 *shutchoh des*
I don't know how long I'll be staying yet	どのぐらい長くいるかまだ分かりません。 *dono-gurigh nagaku iru-ka mada wakarimasen*
I'll be staying here for a weekend	この週末だけいます。 *kono shoo-mats dakay imas*
– for a few days _____	二、三日います。 *ni, san-nichi imas*
– for a week_____	一週間います。 *i-shookan imas*
– for two weeks _____	二週間います。 *ni-shookan imas*
I've got nothing to declare	何も申告する物はありません。 *nani-mo shinkoku suru mono-wa arimasen*
I've got...with me_____	…を持っています。 *... o mottay imas*
– ...100 cigarettes_____	たばこは百本あります。 *tabako-wa hyappon arimas*
– ...1 bottle of... _____	…は一本あります。 *... wa ippon arimas*
– some souvenirs _____	二、三のおみやげがあります。 *ni, san-no omiyagay-nga arimas*
These are personal effects	これは自分で使う物です。 *koray-wa jibun-de tsukau mono des*
These are not new _____	これは新しくありません。 *koray-wa ata-rashiku arimasen*
Here's the receipt _____	領収書です。 *ryohshoo-sho des*

How much import duty ___ do I have to pay?	輸入税はいくらですか。
	yunyoo-zay-wa ikura des-ka
Can I go now? _____	行ってもいいですか。
	ittay-mo ee des-ka

5.3 Luggage

Porter! _____	ポーターさん！
	pohtah-san
Could you take this _____ luggage to...?	この荷物を…に持って行って下さい。
	kono nimots-o ... ni mottay ittay kuda-sigh
How much do I _____ owe you?	いくらですか。
	ikura des-ka
Where can I find a_____ luggage trolley?	台車はどこにありますか。
	dighsha-wa doko-ni arimas-ka
Could you store this _____ luggage for me?	この荷物を預かってもらえますか。
	kono nimots-o azukattay mo-rae-mas-ka
Where are the luggage ___ lockers?	ロッカーはどこですか。
	rokkah-wa doko des-ka
I can't get the locker _____ open	ロッカーが空きません。
	rokkah-ga akimasen
How much is it per _____ item per day?	一日一個いくらですか。
	ichinichi ikko ikura des-ka
This is not my _____ bag/suitcase	私のカバンではありません。
	watashi-no kaban de wa arimasen
There's one bag/_____ suitcase missing still	カバンが一つ足りません。
	kaban-ga hitots tarimasen
My suitcase is damaged ___	カバンが壊れています。
	kaban-ga kowarete-imasu

5.4 The car

See the diagram on page 45.

An international driving licence is required to drive in Japan. Traffic drives on the left as in the UK. The speed limit varies but is usually around 40 kph in urban areas and 80 kph on highways; it is 100 kph on expressways. Driving can be complicated because except on some of the expressways signs are written in Japanese characters. Expressways are expensive, and there are in addition many toll roads, especially in scenic areas.

The parts of a car
(the diagram shows the numbered parts)

1 battery	バッテリー	batteree
2 rear light	バック・ライト	bakku-right
3 rear-view mirror	バック・ミラー	bakku-mirah
reversing light	バックアップ・ライト	bakku-upp-right
4 aerial	アンテナ	antena
car radio	ラジオ	rajio
5 petrol tank	燃料タンク／ガソリン・タンク	nenryoh- tanku/gasorin-tanku
6 sparking plugs	スパーク・プラグ	spahk puragu
fuel filter/pump	燃料フィルター／ポンプ	nenryoh firutah/pomp
7 wing mirror	サイド・ミラー	sighdo-mirah
8 bumper	バンパー	banpah
carburettor	キャブレター	kyaburetah
crankcase	クランク・ケース	krank-kays
cylinder	シリンダー	shirindah
ignition	イグニッション	igunishon
warning light	警告灯	kay-koku-toh
dynamo	発電器	hats-den-ki
accelerator	アクセル	akuseru
handbrake	ハンドブレーキ	hando-burayki
valve	弁／バルブ	ben/barubu
9 silencer	マフラー／消音器	mufurah/shoh-on-ki
10 boot	トランク	toranku
11 headlight	ヘッド・ライト	heddo-right
crank shaft	クランクシャフト	kurank-shafuto
12 air filter	エア・フィルター	e-a firutah
fog lamp	フォグ・ランプ	fog-rampu
13 engine block	エンジン	enjin
camshaft	カムシャフト	kamu-shafuto
oil filter/pump	オイル・フィルター／ポンプ	oyru-firutah/pomp
dipstick	オイルゲージ	oyru-gayji
pedal	ペダル	pedaru
14 door	ドア	do-a
15 radiator	ラジエーター	raji-aytah
16 brake disc	ブレーキ・ディスク	burayk-disk
spare wheel	スペア・タイヤ	supe-a tigh-a
17 indicator	方向指示器	hohkoh-shijiki
18 windscreen wiper	ワイパー	wigh-pah
19 shock absorbers	ショック・アブソーバー	shokk-absohbah
sunroof	サンルーフ	sanroof
spoiler	スポイラー	spoy-rah
starter motor	スターターモーター	stahtah-mohtah
20 steering column	ステアリング・コラム	stearing-koram
21 exhaust pipe	排気管	high-ki-kan
22 seat belt	シートベルト	sheet-beruto
fan	ファン	fan
23 distributor cables	ディストリビューター・ケーブル	distribyutah kayburu
24 gear lever	シフト・レバー	shift-rebah

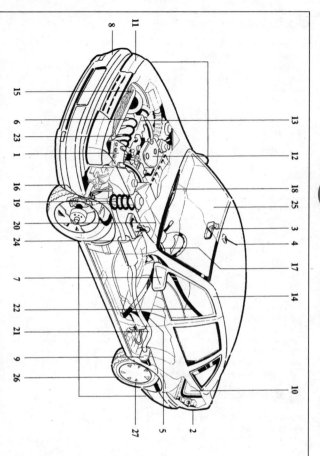

25	windscreen	フロントガラス	*fronto-garas*
	water pump	ウォーターポンプ	*wohtah-pomp*
26	wheel	タイヤ	*tigh-yah*
27	hubcap	ハブ・キャップ	*hab-kyapp*
	piston	ピストン	*piston*

5.5 The petrol station

How many kilometres ____ to the next petrol station, please?	次のガソリン・スタンドまで何キロぐらいですか。
	tsugi-no gasorin-sutando-maday nankiro gurigh des-ka
I would like...litres of..., ____ please	…を…リットルお願いします。
	... o ...rittoru onegigh-shimas
– super ____	ハイオク
	high-oku
– leaded ____	有鉛
	yoo-en
– unleaded ____	無鉛
	mu-en
– diesel ____	ディーゼル
	dee-zeru
I would like...yen's ____ worth of petrol, please	…円だけガソリンお願いします。
	...en dakay gasorin o-negigh-shimas
Fill her up, please ____	満タンお願いします。
	mantan o-negigh-shimas
Could you check...? ____	…を点検して下さい。
	... o tenken shitay kuda-sigh
– the oil level ____	オイル
	oyru
– the tyre pressure ____	タイヤの空気圧
	tighya-no kooki-ats
Could you change ____ the oil, please?	オイルを替えてくれますか。
	oyru-o ka-etay kuremas-ka
Could you clean the ____ windows/the windscreen, please?	(フロント)ガラスをふいてくれますか。
	(fronto) garas-o fu-itay kuremas-ka
Could you give the ____ car a wash, please?	洗車お願いします。
	sensha o-negigh-shimas

5.6 Breakdown and repairs

I'm having car trouble. Could you give me a hand?	車が故障しました。手伝ってください ませんか。
	kuruma-nga koshoh shimashta. tetsu-dattay kudasa-e-masen-ka
I've run out of petrol ____	ガソリンがないんですが
	gasorin-ga nigh-n des-nga
I've locked the keys ____ in the car	鍵を車の中に忘れてしまいました。
	kagi-o kuruma-no naka-ni wasuretay shima-imashta
The car/motorbike/ ____ moped won't start	エンジンがかかりません。
	enjin-nga kakarimasen
Could you call a garage ____ for me, please?	修理屋を呼んでくれませんか。
	shoori-ya-o yonday kuremasen-ka
Could you give me ____ a lift to...?	…まで乗せて下さいませんか。
	... maday nosetay kudasa-e-masen-ka
– a garage? ____	修理屋
	shoori-ya
– into town? ____	町
	machi
– a phone booth? ____	電話ボックス
	denwa boks

Can we take my bicycle?	自転車も持って行けますか。 *jitensha-mo mottay ikemas-ka*
– scooter	スクーターも持って行けますか。 *skootah-mo mottay ikemas-ka*
Could you tow me to a garage?	修理屋まで車を運んで下さいませんか。 *shoori-ya-maday kuruma-o hakonday kudasa-e-masen-ka*
There's probably something wrong with... (See 5.4 and 5.7)	…が悪いんですが。 *... ga warui-n des-nga*
Can you fix it?	修理できますか。 *shoori dekimas-ka*
Could you fix my tyre?	タイヤを修理して下さい。 *tigh-ya-o shoori shtay kuda-sigh*
Could you change this wheel?	このタイヤを交換して下さい。 *kono tigh-ya-o kohkan shtay kuda-sigh*
Can you fix it so it'll get me to...?	…へ行けるまでの修理をお願いできますか。 *... e ikeru maday-no shoori-o onegigh-deki mas-ka*
Which garage can help me?	どの修理屋で修理出来ますか。 *dono shoori-ya-de shoori dekimas-ka*
When will my car/bicycle be ready?	いつ取りに来れますか。 *its tori-ni koremas-ka*
Can I wait for it here?	ここで待てますか。 *koko-de matemas-ka*
How much will it cost?	いくらかかりますか。 *ikura kakarimas-ka*
Could you itemise the bill?	勘定を明細に書いて下さい。 *kanjoh-o maysigh-ni kigh-tay kuda-sigh*
Can I have a receipt for the insurance?	保険のための領収書を下さい。 *hoken-no tamay-no ryohshoo-sho-o kuda-sigh*

5 .7 The bicycle/moped

See the diagram on page 49.

The bicycle is used by large numbers of commuters to get to stations and by housewives shopping in the local shopping districts. Because the roads are considered dangerous, most cyclists use footpaths; cycle paths are rare. Bicycles can be hired by the hour or day at most tourist centres, usually near the main station, and provide a convenient way to do sightseeing, cycle maps being provided.

The parts of a bicycle
(the diagram shows the numbered parts)

1 rear lamp	バック・ライト	*bakku right*
2 rear wheel	後車輪	*koh-sharin*
3 (luggage) carrier	荷台	*ni-digh*
4 bicycle fork	フォーク	*fohk*
5 bell	ベル	*beru*
inner tube	チューブ	*choob*
tyre	タイヤ	*tigh-ya*
6 crank	クランク	*kurank*
7 gear change	変速機	*hen-soku-ki*
wire	ワイヤー	*wigh-ya*
dynamo	発電器	*hatsu-denki*
frame	フレーム	*fraym*
8 dress guard	泥除け	*doro-yokay*
9 chain	チェーン	*chayn*
chain guard	チェーン・カバー	*chayn kabah*
milometer	走行距離計	*sohkoh kyohri-kay*
child's seat	子供用いす	*kodomo-yoh isu*
10 headlamp	ヘッドランプ	*heddo ramp*
bulb	電球	*den-kyoo*
11 pedal	ペダル	*pedaru*
12 pump	空気入れ	*kooki-iray*
13 reflector	反射鏡	*hansha-kyoh*
14 brake pad	ブレーキ・ブロック	*burayk-brok*
15 brake cable	ブレーキ・ケーブル	*burayk kayburu*
16 ring lock	キー	*kee*
17 carrier straps	荷台ロープ	*nidigh-rohp*
tachometer	スピード・メーター	*speedo-mehtah*
18 spoke	スポーク	*spohk*
19 mudguard	泥よけ	*doro-yokay*
20 handlebar	ハンドル	*handoru*
21 chain wheel	チェーン・ホイール	*chayn hweeru*
toe clip	トウクリップ	*toh-kuripp*
22 crank axle	クランク軸	*kurank-jiku*
drum brake	ドラム・ブレーキ	*doram-burayk*
rim	リム	*rimu*
23 valve	チューブ	*choob*
24 valve tube	タイヤバルブ	*tigh-ya barubu*
25 gear cable	ギア・ケーブル	*geeya kayburu*
26 fork	フォーク	*fohk*
27 front wheel	前車輪	*zen-sharin*
28 seat	サドル	*sadoru*

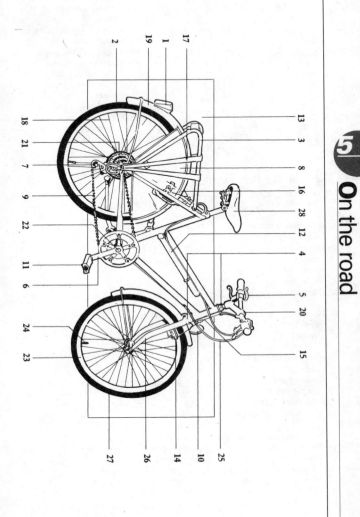

この自動車／自転車の部品はありません。	I don't have parts for your car/bicycle
部品はどこか他へ取りに行かなければなりません。	I have to get the parts from somewhere else
部品を注文しなければなりません。	I have to order the parts
半日かかります。	That'll take half a day
一日かかります。	That'll take a day
二、三日かかります。	That'll take a few days
一週間かかります。	That'll take a week
全損です。	Your car is a write-off
全然修理出来ません。	It can't be repaired
…時に自動車／バイク／オートバイ／自転車を取りに来れます。	The car/motorbike/moped/bicycle will be ready at... o'clock

5.8 Renting a vehicle

I'd like to rent a...	…を借りたいんですが。 ... o karitigh-n des-nga
Do I need a (special) licence for that?	(特別の)運転免許証がいりますか。 (tokubets no) unten menkyoshoh-ga irimas-ka
I'd like to rent the... for...	…借りたいんですが。 ... kari-tigh-n-des-nga
– one day	一日 ichi-nichi
– two days	二日 futsuka
How much is that per day?	一日いくらですか？ ichi-nichi ikura des-ka
– week?	一週間いくらですか？ is-shookan ikura des-ka
How much is the deposit?	保証金はいくらですか？ hoshoh-kin-wa ikura des-ka
Could I have a receipt for the deposit?	保証金の領収書お願いします。 hoshoh-kin-no ryoh-shoo-sho o-negigh-shimas
How much is the surcharge per kilometre?	キロメートルにつき追加料金はいくらですか？ kirometoru-ni-tsuki tsuika-ryohkin-wa ikura des-ka
Does that include petrol?	ガソリン代は入っていますか。 gasorin-digh-wa high-tay imas-ka
Does that include insurance?	保険は含まれていますか。 hoken-wa fuku-maretay imas-ka
What time can I pick the...up tomorrow?	明日何時に取りにこれますか。 ashta nanji-ni tori-ni koremas-ka
When does the...have to be back?	何時までに戻せばいいですか。 nanji maday-ni modoseba ee des-ka

Where's the petrol tank? ___	タンクはどこですか。
	tank-wa doko des-ka
What sort of fuel _____ does it take?	ガソリンは何ですか。
	gasorin-wa nan-des-ka

5.9 Hitchhiking

Hitchhiking is rare in Japan, but foreign tourists sometimes do it.

Where are you heading? ___	どこへ行きますか。
	doko-e ikimas-ka
Can I come along? _____	乗せて下さいますか。
	nosetay kudasa-e-mas-ka
Can my friend come too? __	友達も乗せて下さいますか。
	tomodachi-mo nosetay kudasa-e-mas-ka
I'm trying to get to..._____	…に行きたいんですが。
	... ni iki-tigh-n des-nga
Is that on the way to...? ____	…と同じ方角ですか。
	... to onaji hoh-gaku des-ka
Could you drop me off...? __	…で下ろして下さい。
	... de oroshtay kuda-sigh
– here? _____	ここ
	koko
– at the...exit? _____	…の出口
	... no deguchi
– in the centre?_____	中心
	chooshin
– at the next intersection?__	次の交差点
	tsugi-no kohsaten
Could you stop here, _____ please?	ここで止めて下さい。
	koko-de tometay kuda-sigh
I'd like to get out here _____	ここで下ろして下さい。
	koko-de oroshtay kuda-sigh
Thanks for the lift _____	ありがとうございました。
	arigatoh goza-imashta

5

On the road

Public transport

6 Public transport

6 .1 In general

Where does this train go to?
この電車はどこへ行きますか。
kono densha-wa doko-e ikimas-ka

Does this boat go to...?
この船は…へ行きますか。
kono funay-wa ... e ikimas-ka

Can I take this bus to...?
このバスは…へ行きますか。
kono bas-wa ... e ikimas-ka

Does this train stop at...?
この電車は…に止まりますか。
kono densha-wa ... ni tomarimas-ka

Is this seat free?
この席は空いていますか。
kono seki-wa ightay imas-ka

– reserved?
これは指定席ですか。
kore-wa shtay-seki des-ka

I've booked..
予約しました
yoyaku shimashta

Could you tell me where I have to get off for... ?
…へ行くには、どこで降りるか教えてください。
... e iku-ni-wa, doko-de oriru-ka oshi-etay kuda-sigh

Could you let me know when we get to...?
…に着いたら教えて下さい。
... ni tsui-tara oshi-etay kuda-sigh

Could you stop at the next stop, please?
次のバス停で下ろして下さい。
tsugi-no bas-tay-de oroshtay kuda-sigh

Where are we now?
今どのへんですか。
ima dono-hen des-ka

Do I have to get off here?
ここで降りなければなりませんか。
koko-de ori-nakereba-narimasen-ka

Have we already passed...?
もう…を通りましたか。
moh ... o tohri-mashta-ka

How long have I been asleep?
私はどのぐらい眠りましたか。
watasi-wa dono gurigh nemuri-mashta-ka

How long does...stop here?
…はここにどのくらい止まっていますか。
... wa koko-ni dono-kurigh tomattay imas-ka

Can I come back on the same ticket?
この切符は往復ですか。
kono kippu-wa ohf-ku des-ka

Can I change on this ticket?
この切符で乗り換えられますか。
kono kippu-de norikae-raremas-ka

How long is this ticket valid for?
この切符はいつまで有効ですか。
kono kippu-wa itsu maday yookoh des-ka

Ticket types

この切符は…ですか。	Is this ticket...?
一等	First class
二等	Second class
片道	Single
往復	Return
喫煙車	Smoking
禁煙車	Non-smoking
窓側の座席	Window
通路側の座席	Aisle
列車の前方	Front
列車の後方	Back
座席	Seat
寝台車	Couchette
上・中・下	Top, middle or bottom
エコノミークラスあるいはビジネスクラス？	Tourist class or business class?
船室あるいは座席？	Cabin or seat?
一人用あるいは二人用？	Single or double?
何人ですか。	How many are travelling?

Destination

どこへ行きますか。	Where are you travelling to?
いつ出発しますか。	When are you leaving?
…に出発します。	Your...leaves at...
乗り換えなければなりません。	You have to change trains
…で降りなければなりません。	You have to get off at...
…経由で行かなければなりません。	You have to travel via...
出発は…です。	The outward journey is on...
帰りは…です。	The return journey is on...
…までに乗船しなければなりません。	You have to be on board by...

Inside the vehicle

切符を見せて下さい。	Your ticket, please
指定席券を見せて下さい。	Your reservation, please
パスポートを見せて下さい。	Your passport, please
座席が違います。	You're in the wrong seat
違った…ですが。	You're on/in the wrong...
これは指定席です。	This seat is reserved
特別料金を払わなければなりません。	You'll have to pay a supplement
…は…分遅れています。	The...has been delayed by...minutes

Where can I buy a ticket?	切符はどこで買えますか。 *kipp-wa doko-de ka-emas-ka*
– make a reservation?	どこで予約出来ますか。 *doko-de yoyaku dekimas-ka*
– book a flight?	飛行機の切符はどこで買えますか。 *shikohki-no kippu-wa doko-de ka-emas-ka*
Could I have a single, please?	片道お願いします。 *katamichi onegigh-shimas*
– a return?	往復お願いします。 *ohfuku onegigh-shimas*
first class	一等車 *ittoh-sha*
second class	二等車 *nitoh-sha*
tourist class	エコノミークラス *ekonomi-kurasu*
business class	ビジネスクラス *bijines-kuras*
I'd like to book a seat	座席を予約したいんです。 *zaseki-o yoyaku shitigh-n des*
– couchette	寝台車を予約したいんです。 *shin-digh-sha-o yoyaku shitigh-n-des*
top/middle/bottom	上／中／下 *weh/naka/shta*
I'd like to book a cabin	船室を予約したいんです。 *senshits-o yoyaku shitigh-n des*
smoking/no smoking	喫煙／禁煙 *kitsu-en/kin(g)-en*
by the window	窓際で *mado-giwa-de*
single/double	一人用／二人用 *shtori-yoh/f-tari-yoh*
at the front/back of the train	列車の前方で／列車の後方で *ressha-no zempoh-de/ressha-no koh-hoh-de*
– of the plane	飛行機の前方で／飛行機の後方で *sh-kohki-no zempoh-de/sh-kohki-no koh-hoh-de*
One car	車は一台です。 *kuruma-wa ichi-digh des*
... bicycles	自転車は…台です。 *jitensha-wa ...digh des*
Do you also have season tickets?	定期券もありますか。 *tayki-ken-mo arimas-ka*

6 **Public transport**

Public transport

6

Where's...?	…はどこですか。
	... wa doko des-ka
Where's the information desk?	案内所はどこですか。
	an-nigh-jo-wa doko des-ka
Where can I find a timetable?	時刻表はどこですか。
	jikoku-hyoh-wa doko des-ka
Where's the...desk?	…の売場はどこですか。
	... no uriba-wa doko des-ka
Do you have a city map with the bus/the underground routes on it?	バスや地下鉄が載っている町の地図はありますか。
	bas-ya chika-tets-ga nottay iru machi-no chizu-wa arimas-ka
Do you have a timetable?	時刻表ありますか。
	jikoku-hyoh arimas-ka
I'd like to confirm my booking for/trip to...	…までの旅行／予約を確かめておきたいんです。
	... maday-no ryokoh/yoyaku-o tashi-kametay oki-tigh-n des
I'd like to cancel my booking for/trip to...	…までの旅行／予約を取り消したいんです。
	... maday-no ryokoh/yoyaku-o torikeshi-tigh-n des
I'd like to change my booking for/trip to...	…までの旅行／予約を変えたいんです。
	... maday-no ryokoh/yoyaku-o ka-e-tigh-n des
Will I get my money back?	払戻しを請求出来ますか。
	ha-righ modoshi-o saykyoo dekimas-ka
I want to go to... How do I get there? (What's the quickest way there?)	…へ行きたいんですが、どのように行きますか（何が一番速いですか）。
	... e iki-tigh-n des-nga, dono-yoh-ni ikimas-ka (nani-ga ichiban ha-yigh des-ka)
How much is a single to...?	…までの片道はいくらですか。
	... maday-no katamichi-wa ikura des-ka
How much is a return to...?	…までの往復はいくらですか。
	... maday-no ohf-ku-wa ikura des-ka
Do I have to pay a supplement?	追加料金を払わなければなりませんか。
	tswee-ka ryohkin-o harawa-nakereba-nari-masen-ka
Can I interrupt my journey with this ticket?	この切符で途中下車が出来ますか。
	kono kippu-de tochoo gesha-ga dekimas-ka
How much luggage am I allowed?	荷物は何キロまで持って行けますか。
	nimots-wa nankiro-maday mottay ikemas-ka
Can I send my luggage in advance?	荷物を宅急便で送れますか。
	nimots-o takkyoo-bin-de okuremas-ka
Does this...travel direct?	この…は直行ですか。
	kono ... wa chokkoh des-ka
Do I have to change? Where?	乗り換えなければなりませんか。どこで
	norikae-nakereba-narimasen-ka, doko-de
Will there be any stopovers?	途中止まりますか。
	tochoo tomarimas-ka

Does the boat call in at ____ any ports on the way?	途中港に寄港しますか。
	tochoo minato-ni kikoh shimas-ka
Does the train/bus _____ stop at...?	この電車（バス）は…に止まりますか。
	kono densha (bas)-wa ... ni tomarimas-ka
Where should I get off? ____	どこで降りなければなりませんか。
	doko-de ori-nakereba-narimasen-ka
Is there a connection _____ to...?	…までの接続はありますか。
	... maday-no setsu-zoku-wa arimas-ka
How long do I have _____ to wait?	どのぐらい待たなければなりませんか。
	dono gurigh mata-nakereba-narimasen-ka
When does...leave? _____	…はいつ出発しますか。
	... wa its shuppats shimas-ka
What time does the _____ next...leave?	次の…は何時に出発しますか。
	tsugi-no ....wa nanji-ni shuppats shimas-ka
What time does the _____ last...leave?	最終の…は何時に出発しますか。
	sigh-shoo-no ... wa nanji-ni shuppats shimas-ka
How long does...take? ____	どのぐらいかかりますか。
	dono-gurigh kakarimas-ka
What time does... _____ arrive in...?	…に何時に着きますか。
	... ni nanji-ni tsukimas-ka
Where does the...to... _____ leave from?	…までの電車はどこから出発しますか。
	... maday-no densha-wa doko-kara shuppats shimas-ka
Is this the train/bus/ _____ boat to...?	これは…までの電車／バス／船ですか。
	koray-wa ... maday-no densha/bas/funay des-ka

.5 Airport

(sidebar) **Public transport**

到着	国際
arrivals	international
出発	国内
departures	domestic

6.6 Trains

● **The railway system in Japan is very well developed**, and managed by Japan Railways (JR) and a large number of private railway companies. Inter-city trains are local (*futsoo*), express (*kyoo-koh*), limited express (*tokkyoo*) and super express (*shinkansen*). Tickets are charged by distance, with surcharges for the category of train, class and seat reservations. Ticket reservations are made at counters called 'green windows' (*midori no madoguchi*). Tickets can be bought from ticket machines and most of these have an English option. The full fare does not have to be paid before the destination. Fare adjustment machines and counters are available. All JR stations show station names written in Japanese with the romanisation below. Useful for travellers is the custom of including the names of the previous and next stations to the left and right underneath the station name.

6.7 Taxis

● **Taxis are expensive, but all are metered and there is no custom of tipping.** Carry the address and phone number of your destination, and a map of the immediate location if possible, to give to the driver. Taxi doors are automated; normally the back kerbside door is the only one used. On arrival, wait for the driver to open the door, and do not close it yourself.

空車	満車	タクシー乗り場
for hire	booked	taxi rank

Taxi _____	タクシー！
	tak-shee
Could you get me a _____ taxi, please?	タクシーを呼んで下さい。
	tak-shee-o yonday kuda-sigh
Where can I find a taxi ___ around here?	タクシー乗り場はどこですか。
	tak-shee noriba-wa doko des-ka
Could you take me to..., ___ please?	…までお願いします。
	... maday o-negigh shimas
– this address _____	この住所
	kono joosho
– the...hotel _____	…ホテル
	... hoteru
– the town/city centre_____	中心地
	choo-shin-chi
– the station _____	駅
	eki
– the airport _____	空港
	koo-koh
How much is the _____ trip to...?	…までいくらですか。
	... maday ikura des-ka

Public transport

How far is it to...?	…まで何キロぐらいですか。 *... maday nan-kiro gurigh des-ka*
I'm in a hurry	急いでいるんですが *iso-iday irun des-nga*
Could you speed up/ slow down a little?	もっと速く／ゆっくり行ってください。 *motto hayaku/yukkuri ittay kuda-sigh*
Could you take a different route?	他の道を取って下さい。 *hoka-no michi-o tottay kuda-sigh*
I'd like to get out here, please	ここで下ろして下さい。 *koko-de oroshtay kuda-sigh*
Here	ここで… *koko-de*
You have to go straight on	…真っ直ぐ行ってください。 *... massugu ittay kuda-sigh*
You have to turn left	…左に曲がって下さい。 *... hidari-ni magattay kuda-sigh*
You have to turn right	…右に曲がって下さい。 *... migi-ni magattay kuda-sigh*
This is it	ここです。 *koko des*
Could you wait a minute for me, please?	ちょっと待ってて下さい。 *chotto mattay-tay kuda-sigh*

6

Public transport

Overnight accommodation

7 **O**vernight accommodation

7 .1 **G**eneral

● **Japan has a great variety of overnight accommodation**. There is a wide range of hotels, from five-star international hotels to business hotels and small local establishments. The cheaper the hotel, the smaller the room and the fewer the facilities. Whatever the grade of hotel, cleanliness should be of high order. Other accommodation, especially in country areas, includes the very expensive luxury *ryokan* (traditional inns) and small, cheaper inns. Inns are a good way to experience the Japanese lifestyle. Rooms are covered with straw mats (*tatami*) and the guest sleeps on a mattress (*futon*) spread on the floor. In some inns meals (Japanese style) are also served in the room. Bathing is generally communal (men's and women's facilities are separated) in a large room containing a sunken bath (very hot) for relaxation and individual taps and stools to wash prior to entering the bath. In rural areas these baths may be *onsen* (hot springs).

Many small inns now operate as *minshuku*, inexpensive accommodation offering two meals. These can be booked through the travel counters at stations and airports. They are a good option especially when travelling in the country. In the last few years a western version called *pension* has also become popular. Camping is not popular, and campsites are few and poor in the way of facilities. Youth hostels, of which there is an extensive network, provide a cheap alternative.

いつまでお泊まりですか。	How long will you be staying?
この用紙に記入して下さい。	Fill in this form, please
パスポートをお願いします。	Could I see your passport?
保証金をお願いします。	I'll need a deposit
前払いでお願いします。	You'll have to pay in advance

My name's...I've made a reservation...	私は…です。部屋の予約をしてあります。 *watashi-wa ... des. heya-no yoyaku-o shtay arimas*
– over the phone	電話で *denwa-de*
– by mail	手紙で *tegami-de*
How much is it per night/week/ month?	一泊／一週間／一ヶ月はいくらですか。 *ippaku/isshookan/ikkagets-wa ikura des-ka*
We'll be staying at least two nights/two weeks	せめて二泊／二週間泊まりたいんですが。 *semetay nihaku/nishookan tomari-tigh-n-des-nga*
We don't know yet	まだ分かりませんが。 *mada wakarimasen-nga*
What time does the gate/door open?	何時に開きますか。 *nanji-ni akimas-ka*

– close? _____	何時に閉まりますか。 *nanji-ni shimarimas-ka*
Could you get me a _____ taxi, please?	タクシーを呼んでくれませんか。 *takshee-o yonday kuremasen-ka*
Is there any mail _____ for me?	私宛の手紙がありますか。 *watshi-atay-no tegami-ga arimas-ka*

7 .2 Camping

See the diagram on page 65.

ご自分で場所を決めて下さい。 _____	You can pick your own site
場所が割り当てられています。 _____	You'll be allocated a site
あなたの場所の番号です。 _____	This is your site number
自動車に貼り付けて下さい。 _____	Stick this on your car, please
このカードをなくさないように。 _____	Please don't lose this card

Where's the manager? _____	管理人はどこですか。 *kanri-nin-wa doko des-ka*
Are we allowed to _____ camp here?	ここでキャンプ出来ますか。 *koko-de kyamp dekimas-ka*
There are...of us and... _____ tents	…人とテント…個です。 *...-nin to tento ....-ko des*
Can we pick our own _____ site?	自分で場所を決めてもいいですか。 *jibun-de basho-o kimetay-mo ee des-ka*
Do you have a quiet _____ spot for us?	静かな場所がありますか。 *shizuka-na basho-ga arimas-ka*
Do you have any other _____ sites available?	他に場所がありませんか。 *hoka-ni basho-ga arimasen-ka*
It's too windy/sunny/ _____ here	ここは風／日ざしが強過ぎます。 *koko-wa kazay/hizashi-ga tsuyo-sugi-mas*
It's too shady here _____	ここは日陰が多過ぎます。 *koko-wa hikagay-ga oh-sugi-mas*
It's too crowded here _____	ここは混み過ぎています。 *koko-wa komi-sugi-tay mas*
The ground's too _____ hard/uneven	地面は堅過ぎます／でこぼこです *jimen-wa kata-sugimas/deko-boko des*
Do you have a level _____ spot for the camper/ caravan/folding caravan?	キャンピングカーのために平らな場所があり ますか。 *kyamping-kah-no tamay-ni tighra-na basho-ga* *arimas-ka*
Could we have _____ adjoining sites?	一緒に立てられる場所がありますか。 *issho-ni tate-rareru basho-ga arimas-ka*
Can we park the car _____ next to the tent?	テントの隣に駐車してもいいですか。 *tento-no tonari-ni choosha shtay-mo ee des-ka*
How much is it per _____ person/tent/caravan/car?	一人／テント一個／キャンピングカー一台／ 車一台はいくらですか。 *shtori/tento ikko/kyamping-kah ichi-digh/* *kuruma ichi-digh-wa ikura des-ka*

Do you have any huts to rent?	貸小屋もありますか。
	kashi-goya-mo arimas-ka
Are there any...?	…ありますか。
	... arimas-ka
– any hot showers?	お湯のシャワー…
	oyu-no shawah
– washing machines?	洗濯機
	sentakki
Is there a...on the site?	キャンプ場に…ありますか。
	kyamp-jo-ni ... arimas-ka
Is there a children's play area on the site?	キャンプ場には、子供用の遊び場が ありますか。
	kyamp-jo-ni-wa kodomoyoh-no asobiba-ga arimas-ka
Can I rent a locker here?	ロッカーが借りられますか。
	rokkah-ga kari-raremas-ka
Are we allowed to barbecue here?	バーベキューをしてもいいですか。
	bahbekyoo-o shtay-mo ee des-ka
Are there any power points?	電気を使えますか。
	denki-o tsuka-emas-ka
Is there drinking water?	飲み水はありますか。
	nomi-mizu wa arimas-ka
When's the rubbish collected?	ごみはいつ集めますか。
	gomi-wa its atsume-mas-ka
Do you sell gas bottles (butane gas/propane gas)?	ガスボンベはありますか。
	gas-bombay-wa arimas-ka

7 .3 Hotel/B&B/apartment/holiday house

Do you have a single available?	一人部屋ありますか。
	shtori-beya arimas-ka
– double room...	二人部屋ありますか。
	ftari-beya arimas-ka
per person/per room	一人に付き／一部屋に付き
	shtori-ni-tski/ hito-heya-ni-tski
Does that include breakfast/lunch/dinner?	朝食／昼食／夕食付きですか。
	choh-shoku/choo-shoku/yoo-shoku tski-mas-ka
Could we have two adjoining rooms?	隣り合わせの部屋ありますか。
	tonari-awase-no heya arimas-ka
with toilet/bath/shower	トイレ／バス／シャワー付きの部屋
	toyray/bas/shawah-tski-no heya
without toilet/bath/ shower	トイレ／バス／シャワーなしの部屋
	toyray/bas/shawah-nashi-no heya
facing the street	道に面している部屋
	michi-ni men-shtay iru heya
not facing the street	道に面していない部屋
	michi-ni men-shtay i-nigh heya
with a view of the sea	海側の部屋
	umi-gawa-no heya
without a view of the sea	海に面していない部屋
	umi-ni men-shtay i-nigh heya
Is there a lift in the hotel?	エレベーターありますか。
	erebehtah arimas-ka
Do you have room service?	ルームサービスありますか。
	room-sahbis arimas-ka
Could I see the room?	部屋を見せてもらえますか。
	heya-o misetay moraemas-ka

Camping equipment
(the diagram shows the numbered parts)

luggage space	荷物置場	nimots-okiba
can opener	かん切り	kan-kiri
butane gas bottle	ブタン・ガスボンベ	butan-gas-bombay
1 pannier	自転車用バッグ	jitensha-yoh baggu
2 gas cooker	ガス・コンロ	gas-konro
3 groundsheet	グランドシート	gurando sheeto
mallet	かなずち	kana-zuchi
hammock	ハンモック	hammok
4 jerry can	燃料タンク	nenryoh-tank
campfire	キャンプファイヤー	kyamp figh-ya
5 folding chair	折りたたみ式キャンプ用いす	oritatami-shki kyamp-yoh isu
6 insulated picnic box	クール・ボックス	kooru bokks
ice pack	アイスパック	ighs-pakku
compass	コンパス	kompas
wick	芯	shin
corkscrew	コルク栓抜き	kork-sen-nuki
7 airbed	エア・マットレス	e-a mattres
8 airbed plug	プラグ	prag
pump	空気入れ	kooki iray
9 awning	日よけ	hi-yokay
10 karimat	マットレス	mattres
11 pan	鍋	nabay
12 pan handle	鍋つかみ	nabay ts-kami
primus stove	コンロ	konro
zip	ファスナー／ジッパー	fasnah/ jippah
13 backpack	リュックサック	ryuk-sakk
14 guy rope	張り網	hari-zuna
sleeping bag	寝袋	ne-bukuro
15 storm lantern	ランタン／灯油ランプ	rantan/ toh-yoo ramp
camp bed	キャンプ用ベッド	kyamp-yoh beddo
table	折りたたみ式（キャンプ用）テーブル	oritatami-shki (kyamp-yoh) tayburu
16 tent	テント	tento
17 tent peg	ペグ	pegg
18 tent pole	テント・ポール	tento-pohru
vacuum flask	魔法瓶	mahohbin
19 water bottle	水筒	sweetoh
clothes peg	洗濯バサミ	sentaku-basami
clothes line	物干しロープ	monohoshi rohp
windbreak	風よけ	kaze-yoke
20 torch	懐中電灯／ポケットライト	kigh-choo den-toh/pokett-right-to
pocket knife	小刀	kogatana

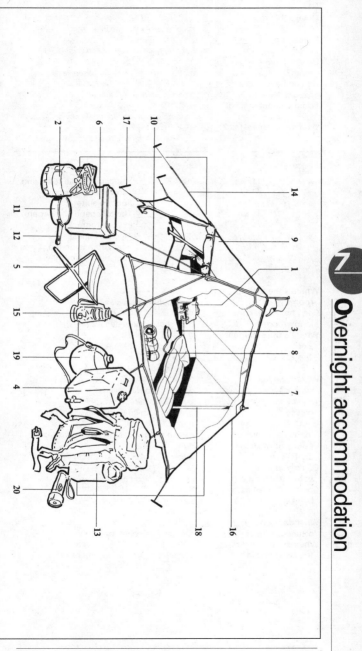

I'll take this room_____	この部屋に決めました。
	kono-heya-ni kime-mashta
Please show us _____ another room	他の部屋を見せて下さい。
	hoka-no heya-o misetay kuda-sigh
Do you have a larger _____ room?	もっと大きい部屋はありませんか。
	motto ohkee heya-wa arimasen-ka
Do you have a less _____ expensive room?	もっと安い部屋はありませんか。
	motto yasui heya-wa arimasen-ka
Could you put in a cot? ____	子供用のベッドを追加できますか。
	kodomo-yoh-no beddo-o tsweeka-dekimas-ka
What time's breakfast? ____	朝食は何時ですか。
	choh-shoku-wa nanji des-ka

トイレやバスは同階／部屋にあります。 _____	You can find the toilet and shower on the same floor/en suite
トイレやバスは部屋にあります。 _____	The toilet and shower are in your room
こちらです。 _____	This way, please
…階にあります。 _____	Your room is on the...floor
部屋番号は…番です。 _____	Your room is number...

Where's the dining _____ room?	食堂はどこですか。
	shokudoh-wa doko des-ka
Can I have breakfast _____ in my room?	朝食を部屋で食べられますか。
	choh-shoku-o heya-de tabe-rare-mas-ka
Where's the emergency ___ exit?	非常口はどこですか。
	hijoh-guchi-wa doko des-ka
– fire escape? _____	非常階段はどこですか。
	hijoh kigh-dan-wa doko des-ka
Where can I park _____ my car?	どこに駐車出来ますか。
	doko-ni choo-sha dekimas-ka
The key to room..., _____ please	…番の部屋の鍵お願いします。
	...ban-no heya-no kagi o-negigh-shimas
Could you put this _____ in the safe, please?	これを金庫に入れて下さいますか。
	koray-o kinko-ni iretay kuda-sigh-mas-ka
Could you wake me _____ at...tomorrow?	明日…時に起こして下さい。
	ashta ...ji-ni okoshtay kuda-sigh
Could you find a _____ babysitter for me?	ベビーシッターがほしいんですが。
	bebee-shitta-ga hoshee-n des-nga
Could I have an extra _____ blanket?	すみませんが、毛布もう一枚お願いします。
	sumimasen-nga, mohfu moh ichi-migh o-negigh-shimas
What days do the _____ cleaners come in?	お掃除は何曜日ですか。
	osohji-wa nanyohbi des-ka
When are the sheets/_____ towels changed?	いつシーツ／タオルを取り替えますか。
	its sheets/taoru-o tori-ka-emas-ka

We can't sleep for _____ the noise	うるさくて眠れないんです。 *uru-sakutay nemure-nigh-n-des*
Could you turn the _____ radio down, please?	ラジオの音量を下げて下さい。 *rajio-no onryo-o sagetay kuda-sigh*
We're out of toilet _____ paper	トイレットペーパーがないんですが。 *toyretto-pehpah-ga naigh-n-des-nga*
There aren't any.../ _____ there's not enough...	…が足りないんです。 *... ga tari-nigh-n-des*
The bed linen's dirty_____	シーツがきたないのですが。 *sheets-ga kita-nigh-no-des-nga*
The room hasn't _____ been cleaned	部屋が掃除してありません。 *heya-ga sohji shtay arimasen*
The heater's not _____ working	暖房が働いていません。 *damboh-ga hatarigh-tay imasen*
The air conditioning's _____ not working	エアーコンが働いていません。 *e-a-kon-ga hatarigh-tay imasen*
There's no water _____	水が出ません。 *mizu-ga demasen*
– hot water _____	お湯が出ません。 *oyu-ga demasen*
– electricity _____	電気がありません。 *denki-ga arimasen*
...is broken_____	…がこわれています。 *... ga kowaretay imas*
Could you have that _____ seen to?	そのようによろしくお願いします。 *sono-yoh-ni yoroshku o-negigh-shimas*
Could I have another _____ room/site?	他の部屋に替えて下さい。 *hoka-no heya-ni ka-etay kuda-sigh*
The bed creaks terribly _____	ベッドがすごい音をたてるんですが。 *beddo-ga sugoi oto-o tateru-n-des-nga*
The bed sags _____	ベッドが柔らか過ぎます。 *beddo-ga yawaraka-sugimas*
There are bugs/insects _____ in our room	部屋に虫がいるんですが。 *heya-ni mushi-ga iru-n-des-nga*
This place is full of... _____	ここには…がたくさんいて、こまります。 *koko-ni-wa ... ga takusan itay, komarimas*
– mosquitos _____	蚊 *ka*
– cockroaches _____	ゴキブリ *go-kiburi*
– Brits _____	イギリス人 *igirisu-jin*

7

Overnight accommodation

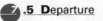

See also 8.2 Settling the bill

I'm leaving tomorrow. Could I settle my bill, please?	明日立ちますから、精算して下さい。 *ashta tachi-mas-kara saysan shtay kuda-sigh*
What time should we vacate?	何時までに部屋をあけなければなりませんか。 *nanji maday-ni heya-o ake-nakereba-nari-masen-ka*
Could I have my deposit/passport back, please?	保証金／パスポートを返して下さい。 *hoshoh-kin/paspohto-o kighshtay kuda-sigh*
We're in a terrible hurry	大変急いでいます。 *tigh-hen isoi-de imas*
Could you forward my mail to this address?	この住所に手紙を回送して下さいますか。 *kono joosho-ni tegami-o kighsoh shtay kuda-sigh-masu-ka*
Could we leave our luggage here until we leave?	出発まで荷物をここに置いていてもいいですか。 *shuppats-maday nimots-o koko-ni oitay itay-mo ee des-ka*
Thanks for your hospitality	おもてなしありがとうございました。 *omotenashi arigatoh go-zigh-mashta*

Overnight accommodation

68

Money matters

8 Money matters

Money matters

● In general, banks are open Monday-Friday 9-3. They are closed on Saturdays, Sundays and national holidays. Travellers' cheques in yen or dollars are easily cashed at banks, but they are not readily acceptable outside the hotels and shops that cater particularly for the international traveller.

8 .1 Banks

Where can I find a _____ bank/an exchange office around here?	この辺に銀行はありますか。 *kono-hen-ni ginkoh-wa arimas-ka*
Where can I find a _____ post office around here?	この辺に郵便局はありますか。 *kono-hen-ni yoobin-kyoku-wa arimas-ka*
Where can I cash this _____ traveller's cheque/giro cheque?	この（旅行用）小切手はどこで現金に替えられますか。 *kono (ryokoh-yoh) kogit-tay-wa doko-de genkin-ni ka-eraremas-ka*
Can I cash this...here? _____	この…はここで現金に替えられますか。 *kono ... wa koko-de genkin-ni ka-eraremas-ka*
Can I withdraw money_____ on my credit card here?	クレジットカードで現金を引き出せますか。 *krejitto-kahdo-de genkin-o hiki-dasemas-ka*
What's the _____ minimum/maximum amount?	最小／最高はいくらですか。 *sigh-shoh/sigh-koh-wa ikura des-ka*
Can I take out less _____ than that?	少しでもいいですか。 *skoshi-demo ee des-ka*
I've had some money transferred here. Has it arrived yet? These are the details of my bank in the UK.	ここにお金を送金してもらいましたが、もう入金されていますか。これはイギリスの銀行の証書です。 *koko-ni o-kanay-o sohkin shtay morigh-mash-ta-nga, moh nyookin saretay imas-ka. koray-wa igirisu-no ginkoh no shoh-sho des*
This is my bank/giro _____ number	これは私の口座番号です。 *koray-wa watashi-no kohza bango des*
I'd like to change some _____ money	お金を両替したいんですが。 *okanay-o ryoh-gae shtigh-n des-nga*
– pounds into yen _____	ポンドを円に *pondo-o yen-ni*
– dollars into yen_____	ドルを円に *doru-o yen-ni*
What's the exchange _____ rate?	為替レートはいくらですか。 *kawasay rayto-wa ikura des-ka*
Could you give me _____ some small change with it?	こまかいお金も入れて下さい。 *komakigh okanay-mo iretay kuda-sigh*
This is not right _____	間違っていると思いますが *machigattay iru-to omoimas-ng*

ここに署名して下さい。	Sign here, please
これに記入して下さい。	Fill this out, please
パスポートを見せて下さい。	Could I see your passport, please?
身分証明書を見せて下さい。	Could I see some identification, please?
バンクカードを見せて下さい。	Could I see your bank card, please?

.2 Settling the bill

Could you put it on my bill?	部屋に付けておいてください。 *heya-ni tsketay oitay kuda-sigh*
Does this amount include service?	サービス料は入っていますか。 *sahbis-ryoh-wa hight-tay imas-ka*
Can I pay by...?	…で払えますか。 *... de harae-mas-ka*
– credit card?	クレジットカード *krejitto-kahdo*
– traveller's cheque?	旅行用小切手 *ryokoh-yoh kogit-tay*
– with foreign currency?	外貨 *gigh-ka*
You've given me too much	おつりが多すぎます。 *otsuri-ga oh-sugimas*
You haven't given me enough change	おつりが少ないのですが。 *otsuri-ga sku-nigh des-nga*
Could you check this again, please?	もう一度確かめてくださいませんか。 *moh ichido tashi-kametay kuda-sigh-masen-ka*
Could I have a receipt, please?	領収書お願いします。 *ryoh-shoo-sho o-negigh-shimas*
I don't have enough money on me	すみませんが、持ち金が足りません。 *sumimasen-nga, mochi-ganay-nga tarimasen*

クレジットカード／旅行用小切手／外貨はご使用になれません。	We don't accept credit cards/traveller's cheques/foreign currency

This is for you	どうぞ。 *dohzo*
Keep the change	とっておいてください。 *tottay oitay kuda-sigh*

Post and telephone

9 Post and telephone

9.1 Post

● **Post offices open 9-5 Monday-Friday**, with cash related facilities available until 3pm. The main offices in each ward are also open on Saturday mornings, 9-12.30. They are closed on Sundays and national holidays. However, they have after-hours services available for designated items, such as foreign mail. You must press the buzzer near the entrance and an attendant will come out to you. The Central Post Office across from Tokyo Station is open 24 hours a day. You can address letters using the English script (*romaji*).

郵便為替	電報
money orders	telegrams
郵便小包み	切手
parcels	stamps

Where's the post office/main post office?	この辺に郵便局(郵便局の本局)はありますか。
	kono-hen-ni yoo-bin-kyoku (yoo-bin-kyoku-no hon-kyoku)-wa arimas-ka
Where's the postbox?	この辺にポストはありますか。
	kono-hen-ni posto-wa arimas-ka
Which counter should I go to...?	…はどの窓口ですか。
	... wa dono mado-guchi des-ka
– to send a fax	ファックス
	fakks
– to change money	現金扱い
	genkin ats-kigh
– to change giro cheques	小切手
	kogitay
– for a Telegraph Money Order?	電信為替
	denshin kawasay
Poste restante	局留め
	kyoku-domay
Is there any mail for me? My name's...	私宛の郵便はありますか。私の名前は…です。
	watashi-atay-no yoobin-wa arimas-ka. watashi-no na-migh-wa ... des

Stamps

What's the postage for a letter to...?	…までの手紙はいくらですか。
	... made-no tegami-wa ikura des-ka
What's the postage for a postcard to...?	…までの葉書はいくらですか。
	... made-no hagaki-wa ikura des-ka
Are there enough stamps on it?	切手は足りますか。
	kittay-wa tarimas-ka
I'd like... ...yen stamps	…円の切手を…枚お願いします。
	...yen-no kittay-o ...migh onegigh-shimas
I'd like to send this express.	これを速達便でお願いします。
	kore-o sokutats-bin-de o-negigh-shimas

– by air mail _____	これを航空便でお願いします。
	kore-o kohkoobin-de o-negigh-shimas
– by registered mail _____	これを書留でお願いします。
	kore-o kaki-tomay-de o-negigh-shimas

Telegram/fax

I'd like to send a _____ telegram to...	…へ電報を送りたいんです。
	... e dempoh-o okuri-tigh-n des
How much is that _____ per word?	一語につきいくらですか。
	ichigo-ni-tski ikura des-ka
This is the text I _____ want to send.	送る電文はこれです。
	okuru denbun-wa koray des
Shall I fill out the _____ form myself?	用紙は自分で記入しましょうか。
	yohshi-wa jibun-de kinyoo shimashoh-ka
Can I make photocopies ___ here?	ここでコピー出来ますか。
	koko-de kopee dekimas-ka
– send a fax here? _____	ここでファックス出来ますか。
	koko-de fakks dekimas-ka
How much is it per _____ page?	一ページはいくらですか。
	ippayji-wa ikura des-ka

9 .2 Telephone

● **Dialling procedures are shown** by diagrams inside phone boxes. Direct international calls can be made from card phones, most green phones and some grey ones. If a phone can be used to dial abroad, the phone box will display a message in English to this effect. However, owing to the abuse of telephone cards for international calls, it may not be possible to use some card phones to dial overseas. The basic unit-cost is 10 yen per minute. Fax machines are widely available.

To dial internationally through an operator, call 0051 (international information service, 0057). Direct dialling is as follows: 001 – country number – area code – local number. The national number of the UK is 44, Ireland 353, Australia 61, New Zealand 64, and Canada and US 1. Omit the 0 from the area code when dialling.

Could I use your _____ phone, please?	あなたの電話を使ってもいいですか。
	anata-no denwa-o tskattay mo ee des-ka
Do you have a _____ (city/region)...phone directory?	電話帳ありますか。
	denwa-choh arimas-ka
Could you find a _____ telephone number for me?	電話番号を調べて下さいませんか。
	denwa-bango-o shirabetay kudasa-i-masen-ka
Where can I get a _____ phone card?	テレホン・カードはどこで買えますか。
	terehon-kahdo-wa doko-de ka-emas-ka
Could you give me...? _____	…を教えてください。
	... o oshietay kuda-sigh
– the number of room... ___	…番の部屋の電話番号
	...ban-no heya-no denwa-bango
– the international _____ access code	国際電話の番号
	kok-sigh denwa-no bango
– the country code for... ___	…の国番号
	... no kuni bango

– the trunk code for... _____	…の市外局番
	... no shi-gigh kyokuban
– the number of... _____	…の電話番号
	... no denwa-bango
Could you check if this _____ number's correct?	この電話番号が正しいかどうか調べてください。
	kono denwa-bango-ga tada-shee-ka. dohka shirabetay kuda-sigh
Can I dial international _____ direct?	外国に直接ダイヤル出来ますか？
	gigh-koku-ni chokusetsu dighru dekimas-ka
Do I have to go through _____ the switchboard?	交換手を通してですか。
	kohkanshu-o tohsh-tay des-ka
Do I have to dial '0' first? __	最初にゼロをまわしますか。
	sigh-sho-ni zero-o mawashimas-ka
Do I have to book _____ my calls?	通話を申し込まなければなりませんか。
	tsoowa-o mohshi-koma-nakereba-narimasen-ka
Could you dial this _____ number for me, please?	この電話番号につないで下さい。
	kono denwa-bango-ni tsunigh-day kuda-sigh
Could you put me _____ through to.../extension..., please?	…番につないでください。
	...ban-ni tsunigh-day kuda-sigh
I'd like to place a _____ reverse-charge call to...	…にコレクトコールで電話をかけたいんですが。
	...ni korekt-kohru-de denwa-o kake-tigh-n des-nga
What's the charge_____ per minute?	一分につきいくらですか。
	ippun-ni-tski ikura des-ka
Have there been any _____ calls for me?	私に電話がありましたか。
	watashi-ni denwa-ga arimashta-ka

The conversation

Hello, this is..._____	もしもし、…です。
	mosh moshi, ... des
Who is this, please? _____	どなたですか。
	donata des-ka
Is this...? _____	…さんですか。
	... san des-ka
I'm sorry, I've dialled the___ wrong number	すみませんが、間違ってダイヤルしました。
	sumimasen-nga, machi-gattay dighru shimashta
I can't hear you _____	電話が遠くて、聞えにくいんですが。
	denwa-ga tohkutay, kikoe-nikui des-nga
Excuse me, I don't _____ speak Japanese	すみませんが、日本語が分かりません。
	sumimasen-ga, nihongo-ga wakarimasen
Is...there please? _____	…さんいらっしゃいますか。
	... san irasha-i-mas-ka
Is there anybody who _____ speaks English?	英語が出来る人いらっしゃいますか。
	aygo-ga dekiru shto irasha-i-mas-ka
Extension..., please_____	…番をお願いします。
	...ban-o o-ne-gigh shimas

Could you ask him/her ____ to call me back?

後で電話をしてくれるようお願いします。

ato-de denwa-o shtay kureru-yoh o-ne-gigh shimas

My name's... ____
My number's...

私の名前は…です。私の電話番号は…です。

watashi-no na-migh-wa ... des. watashi-no denwa-bango-wa ... des

Could you tell him/her ____ I called?

私が電話をかけたと伝えて下さい。

watashi-wa denwa-o kaketa-to tsuta-etay kuda-sigh

I'll call back tomorrow ____

明日また電話をかけます。

ashta mata denwa-o kakemas

電話です。 ____	There's a phone call for you
最初に0をダイヤルしてください。 ____	You have to dial '0' first
ちょっと待って下さい。 ____	One moment, please
通じません。 ____	There's no answer
話し中です。 ____	The line's engaged
番号が違っています。 ____	You've got a wrong number
今留守です。 ____	He's/she's not here right now
…時に戻ります。 ____	He'll/she'll be back at...

Shopping

10 Shopping

● **Shops usually open around 10am and close around 8pm**.
Department stores close between 6pm and 7pm, depending on the
store and the day. All shops close one day per week. Neighbourhood
shops, with the exception of supermarkets, tend to close on Sundays.
Large department stores are always open on Saturdays and Sundays,
but close for one day during the week except at busy times in July and
December. 'Convenience stores' which remain open 24 hours a day can
now be found in most urban localities. Discount stores offer
mainstream goods at up to 40% cheaper than the department stores.
There is a sales tax of 5% on all items; this is added to the final bill and
is not included in the price displayed. Bargaining is not the norm in
Japan, and attempts to do so will generally be met by a flat refusal. It
is customary for shop assistants to greet customers with the greeting
irasshaimase (welcome).

department store	デパート	*depahto*
antiques	骨董店／アンチーク	*kottoh-ten/ancheek*
household goods	雑貨屋	*zakka-ya*
camera shop	写真屋	*shashinya*
sports shop	スポーツ用品店	*spohts yoh-hin-ten*
second-hand goods	古物屋	*furumono-ya*
bicycle shop	自転車屋	*jitensha-ya*
liquor shop	酒屋	*sakaya*
shoe shop	靴屋	*kuts-ya*
butcher	肉屋	*nikuya*
shopping arcade	商店街	*shohten-gigh*
delicatessen	総菜屋／ デリカテッセン	*sohzigh-ya/ derikatessen*
food shop	食料品店	*shokuryoh-hin-ten*
cake shop	ケーキ屋	*kayki-ya*
electrical appliances	電気屋	*denkiya*
tobacconist	タバコ屋	*tabakoya*
(dispensing) chemist	薬局	*yak-kyoku*
hardware shop	金物屋	*kanamono-ya*
florist	花屋	*hanaya*
grocery store	八百屋	*ya-oya*
greengrocer	果物屋	*kudamono-ya*
jeweller	貴金属店／宝石店	*kikinzoku-ten/hohseki-ten*
toy shop	おもちゃ屋	*omocha-ya*
laundry	洗濯屋	*sentaku-ya*
launderette	コインランドリー	*koyn rahnderee*
bookshop	本屋	*honya*
market	市場／マーケット	*ichiba/mahketto*
optician	眼鏡屋	*megane-ya*
bakery	パン屋	*panya*
beauty parlour	美容院	*biyoh-in*
hairdresser	床屋	*toko-ya*
perfume shop	香水店	*kohswee-ten*
fishmonger	魚屋	*sakana-ya*

Shopping

English	Japanese	Romanization
kiosk	キオスク／売店	kiosk / bigh-ten
souvenir shop	みやげ物店	miyage-mono-ten
bicycle repairs	自転車屋	jitensha-ya
supermarket	スーパー	soopah
shop	店	misay
record shop	レコード屋	rekohdo-ya
leather shop	毛皮専門店	kegawa-semmon-ten
clothes shop	洋品店	yoh-hin-ten
dairy	牛乳屋	gyoo-nyoo-ya
china wear	瀬戸物屋	setomono-ya
sweet shop	お菓子屋	okashi-ya
DIY-store	日曜大工店	nichiyoh-dighku-ten
dry-cleaner	クリーニング屋	kureening-ya
fleamarket	のみの市	nomino-ichi
health food shop	健康食料品店	kenkoh-shokuryoh-hin-ten

🔟 .1 Shopping conversations

Where can I get...? _____
…はどの店にありますか。
... wa dono mise-ni arimas-ka

When does this shop _____ open?
この店はいつ開きますか。
kono mise-wa its akimas-ka

Could you tell me _____ where the...department is?
…売場はどこですか。
... uriba-wa doko des-ka

Could you help me, _____ please? I'm looking for...
すみませんが、…がほしいんですが。
sumimasen-nga, ... ga hoshee-n des-nga

Do you sell English/ _____ American newspapers?
英語の新聞もありますか。
eigo-no shimbun-mo arimas-ka

...please _____
…を下さい。
... o kuda-sigh

I'm just looking _____
ちょっと見ているだけです。
chotto mite-iru dakay des

I'd also like..._____
…も下さい。
... mo kuda-sigh

Could you show me...? ____
…を見せて下さい。
... o misetay kuda-sigh

Do you have _____ something...?
…のはありませんか。
... no-wa arimasen-ka

– less expensive?_____
もっと安い
motto ya-sui

– something smaller?_____
もっと小さい
motto chee-sigh

– something larger? _____
もっと大きい
motto oh-kee

I'll take this one _____
これ下さい。
koray kuda-sigh

Does it come with _____ instructions?
説明書は入っていますか。
setsumaysho-wa hight-tay imas-ka

It's too expensive _____
ちょっと高過ぎます。
chotto taka-sugimas

Shopping

🔟

Could you keep this _____ for me? I'll come back for it later	あずかって下さいませんか。あとで取りに来ます。
	azukattay kudasa-i-masen-ka. ato-de tori-ni kimas
Have you got a bag _____ for me, please?	ビニール袋ありますか。
	bineeru bukuro arimas-ka
Could you giftwrap it, _____ please?	プレゼントですから、包んで下さい。
	prezento des-kara, ts-tsunday kuda-sigh

すみませんが、ありません。 _____	I'm sorry, we don't have that
すみませんが、売切れです。 _____	I'm sorry, we're sold out
支払い所でお支払いください。 _____	You can pay at the cash desk
クレジットカードは使えません。 _____	We don't accept credit cards
旅行用小切手は使えません。 _____	We don't accept traveller's cheques
外貨は使えません。 _____	We don't accept foreign currency

🔟 .2 Food

I'd like a hundred _____ grams of..., please	…を100グラムお願いします。
	... o hyaku gram o-negigh-shimas
– five hundred grams/ _____ half a kilo of...	…を500グラム
	... o gohyaku-gram
– a kilo of... _____	…を1キロ
	... o ichi-kiro
Could you...it for me, _____ please?	…下さい。
	... kuda-sigh
Could you slice it/dice _____ it for me, please?	薄く／さいの目に切って下さい。
	usuku/sigh-nomay-ni kittay kuda-sigh
Could you grate it _____ for me, please?	おろして下さい。
	oroshtay kuda-sigh
Can I order it? _____	注文出来ますか。
	choomon dekimas-ka
I'll pick it up _____ tomorrow/at...	あした／…時に取りに来ます。
	ashta/... ji-ni tori-ni kimas
Can you eat this? _____	食べ物ですか。
	tabemono des-ka
Can you drink this? _____	飲み物ですか。
	nomimono des-ka
What's in it? _____	材料は何ですか。
	zigh-ryoh-wa nan des-ka

I'd like something to _____ go with this	何かこれに似合うのがほしいんですが。
	nani-ka kore-ni ni-au-no-ga hoshee-n des-nga
Do you have shoes to _____ match this?	これに似合う靴がありますか。
	kore-ni ni-au kuts-ga arimas-ka
I'm a size...in the UK_____	イギリスの…サイズなんですが。
	igirisu-no ... sighz nan des-nga
Can I try this on? _____	試着出来ますか。
	shi-chaku dekimas-ka
Where's the fitting _____ room?	試着室はどこですか
	shi-chaku-shits-wa doko des-ka
It doesn't fit_____	このサイズは合いません。
	kono sighz-wa igh-masen
This is the right size _____	このサイズは大丈夫です。
	kono sighz-wa digh-johbu des
It doesn't suit me_____	似合いません。
	ni-igh imasen
The heel's too high/low ____	かかとが高過ぎます／低過ぎます。
	kakato-ga taka-sugimas / hiku-sugimas
Is this/are these _____ genuine leather?	これは本当の皮ですか。
	kore-wa hontoh-no kawa des-ka
I'm looking for a...for a three-year-old child	3歳の子供のために…がほしいんですが。
	san-sigh-no kodomo-no tame-ni ... ga hoshee-n des-nga
I'd like a silk... _____	絹の…お願いします。
	kinu-no ... o-negigh shimas
– cotton... _____	木綿の…お願いします。
	momen-no ... o-negigh shimas
– woollen... _____	ウールの…お願いします。
	wooru-no ... o-negigh shimas
– linen... _____	麻の…お願いします。
	asa-no ... o-negigh shimas
What temperature can I wash it at?	洗濯温度は何度ですか。
	sentaku ondo-wa nando des-ka
Will it shrink in the _____ wash?	洗ったら、縮みますか。
	arat-tara, chijimi-mas-ka

Shopping
10

濡れたまま干して下さい。	洗濯機で洗えます。	アイロンをかけないで下さい。
Drip dry	**Machine wash**	**Do not iron**
手で洗って下さい。	ドライクリーニングにして下さい。	
Hand wash	**Dry clean**	

At the cobbler

Could you mend _____ these shoes?	この靴を修理出来ますか。
	kono kutsu-o, shoori dekimas-ka
Could you put new _____ soles/heels on these?	新しい靴底／かかとを作ってください。
	atara-shee kuts-zoko/kakato-o ts-kuttay kuda-sigh
When will they be _____ ready?	いつできますか♪
	its dekimas-ka

I'd like..., please	…お願いします。
	... o-negigh shimas
– a tin of shoe polish	靴クリーム
	kuts-kreem
– a pair of shoelaces	靴ひも
	kutsu-himo

10.4 Photographs and video

I'd like...	…下さい。
	... kuda-sigh
– a film	フィルム
	firum
– black and white film	黒白フィルム
	kuro-shiro firum
– colour film	カラーフィルム
	karah-firum
– a slide film	スライドフィルム
	srighd-firum
– a cartridge	カセットフィルム
	kasetto-firum
– a videotape	ビデオテープ
	bideo-tehp
– an 8mm film	8ミリ映画用フィルム
	hachi-miri ayga-yoh firum
12/24/36 exposures	12枚撮り／24枚撮り／36枚撮りのフィルム
	joo-ni-migh dori/nijoo-yon-migh dori/san joo-roku-migh dori no firum
ASA/DIN number	ASA/DIN 番号
	ay-ess-ay/dee-igh-en bango
daylight film	昼光用のフィルム
	chukoh-yoh-no firum
film for artificial light	人工光用のフィルム
	jinkohkoh-yoh-no firum

Problems

Could you load the film for me, please?	このカメラにフィルムを入れて下さい。
	kono kamera-ni firum-o iretay kuda-sigh
Could you take the film out for me, please?	フィルムを取り出して下さい。
	firum-o tori-dashtay kuda-sigh
Should I replace the batteries?	バッテリーを取り換えなければなりませんか。
	batteree-o tori-kae-nakereba-narimasen-ka
Could you have a look at my camera, please? It's not working	このカメラを見てくれませんか。使えなくなってしまいました。
	kono kamera-o mitay kuremasen-ka. tsuka-enaku-nattay shimaimashta
The...is broken	…がこわれました。
	... ga kowaremashta
The film's jammed	フィルムが動きません。
	firum-ga ugoki-masen
The film's broken	フィルムが切れました。
	firum-ga kiremashta
The flash isn't working	フラッシュが点灯しません。
	furash-ga tentoh shimasen

Processing and prints

I'd like to have this _____ film developed, please
このフィルムを現像してください。
kono firum-o genzoh shtay kuda-sigh

– printed, please _____
このフィルムをプリントしてください。
kono firum-o print shtay kuda-sigh

I'd like...prints from _____ each negative
このネガを…枚ずつプリントして下さい。
kono nega-o ... migh-zuts print shtay kuda-sigh

glossy/mat _____
光沢のある／光沢のない
kohtaku-no aru / kohtaku-no nigh

I'd like to have this _____ photo enlarged
これを引き伸ばして下さい。
kore-o hiki-nobashtay kuda-sigh

How much is...? _____
…はいくらですか。
... wa ikura des-ka

– processing? _____
現像
genzoh

– printing _____
プリント
print

– the enlargement _____
引き伸ばし
hiki-nobashi

When will they be _____ ready?
いつできますか。
its dekimas-ka

🔟 .5 At the hairdresser's

Do I have to make _____ an appointment?
予約しなければなりませんか。
yoyak shi-nakereba narimasen-ka

How long will I _____ have to wait?
どのぐらい待ちますか。
dono gurigh machimas-ka

I'd like a... _____
髪を…下さい。
kami-o ... kuda-sigh

– shampoo _____
洗って
arattay

– haircut _____
切って
kittay

I'd like a shampoo _____ for... please
…用のシャンプーお願いします。
... yoh-no shampoo o-negigh shimas

– oily hair _____
あぶらの多い髪
abura-no oh-ee kami

– dry hair _____
あぶらの少ない髪
abura-no sku-nigh kami

– a shampoo for _____ permed hair
パーマをかけた髪
pahm-o kaketa kami

– a shampoo for _____ coloured hair
染まった髪
somatta kami

I'd like an anti-dandruff _____ shampoo
ふけ防止用のシャンプーお願いします。
f-kay bohshi-yoh-no shampoo o-negigh shimas

– a colour rinse _____ shampoo
カラーシャンプーお願いします。
karah shampoo o-negigh shimas

I want to keep it the same colour	この色と同じにして下さい。 *kono iro-to onaji-ni shtay kuda-sigh*
I'd like it darker/lighter	もっと黒く／明るくして下さい。 *motto kuroku/akaruku shtay kuda-sigh*
I'd like...	…をかけてください。 *... o kaketay kuda-sigh*
I don't want...	…はかけないで下さい。 *... wa kake-nigh-day kuda-sigh*
– hair spray	ヘアスプレー *he-a spray*
– gel	ジェル *jeru*
– lotion	ローション *rohshon*
I'd like a short fringe	前髪を短く切って下さい。 *ma-e-gami-o miji-kaku kittay kuda-sigh*
Not too short at the back	後は短過ぎないように *ushiro-wa mijika-sugi-nigh yoh-ni*
Not too long here	ここは長過ぎないように *koko-wa naga-sugi-nigh yoh-ni*
It needs a little taken off	少しだけ切って下さい。 *skoshi dakay kittay kuda-sigh*
I want a completely different style	他の髪型にしたいんです。 *hoka-no kamigata-ni shitigh-n des*
I'd like it the same...	…のような髪型にしたいんですが… *... no yoh-na kamigata-ni shitigh-n des-nga*
– as that lady's	あの方 *ano kata*
– as in this photo	この写真 *kono shashin*
Could you put the drier up a bit?	ドライヤーを高くして下さい。 *drighyah-o takaku shtay kuda-sigh*
Could you put the drier down a bit?	ドライヤーを低くして下さい。 *drighyah-o hikuku shtay kuda-sigh*
I'd like...	…をして下さい。 *... o shtay kuda-sigh*
– a manicure	マニキュア *manikyua*
– a massage	マッサージ *massahji*

どんな髪型がいいんですか。	What style did you have in mind?
どんな色がいいんですか。	What colour did you want it?
温度はよろしいですか。	Is the temperature all right for you?
雑誌をお読みになりますか。	Would you like something to read?
何かお飲みになりますか。	Would you like a drink?
これでよろしいですか。	Is this what you had in mind?

Could you trim...	…を切りそろえて下さい。
	... o kiri-soroetay kuda-sigh
– my fringe?	前髪
	ma-e-gami
– my beard?	ひげ
	higay
– my moustache?	口ひげ
	kuchi-higay
I'd like a shave, please	ひげを剃って下さい。
	hige-o sottay kuda-sigh
I'd like a wet shave, please	ひげ剃り用カミソリで剃って下さい。
	hige-sori-yoh kamisori-de sottay kuda-sigh

At the Tourist Information Centre

 **A**t the Tourist Information Centre

The Japan National Tourist Office (JNTO) provides information in English in Tokyo and Kyoto and at Narita Airport. There is also a Travel Phone service offering tourist information and language assistance in English during business hours. In smaller places, information centres are usually located at the railway station.

11 .1 **P**laces of interest

Most museums, tourist sites and nationally famous temples and gardens charge entrance fees, which average around 400–600 yen for adults. If possible, wear shoes that can be slipped on and off easily, since many tourist attractions, particularly temples and old buildings, require shoes to be removed at the entrance.

Where's the Tourist Information centre, please?	観光案内所はどこですか。 *kankoh an-nigh-sho-wa doko des-ka*
Do you have a city map?	町の地図ありますか。 *machi-no chizu arimas-ka*
Could you give me some information about...?	…について教えて下さい。 *... ni tsuitay oshietay kuda-sigh*
How much is that?	いくらですか。 *ikura des-ka*
What are the main places of interest?	主にどこが面白いですか。 *omo-ni doko-ga omoshiro-i des-ka*
Could you point them out on the map?	地図で指して下さい。 *chizu-de sashtay kuda-sigh*
What do you recommend?	何かおすすめは。 *nani-ka osusume-wa*
We'll be here...	ここに…います。 *koko-ni ... imas*
– for a few hours	二、三時間 *ni, san jikan*
– a day	一日 *ichi-nichi*
– a week	一週間 *is-shoo-kan*
We're interested in...	…に興味があJますŧŦが。 *... ni kyohmi-ga arimas-ga*
Is there a scenic walk around the city?	市内観光ありますか。 *shinigh kankoh arimas-ka*
How long does it take?	どのぐらい時間がかかりますか。 *dono gurigh jikan-ga kakarimas-ka*
Where does it start/end?	出発点／終点はどこですか。 *shuppats-ten/shooten-wa doko des-ka*
Are there any boat cruises here?	遊覧船がありますか。 *yooransen ga arimas-ka*
Where can we board?	どこで船に乗れますか。 *doko-de fune-ni noremas-ka*
Are there any bus tours?	観光バスがありますか。 *kankoh bas ga arimas-ka*

11

Where do we get on?	どこでバスに乗れますか。	*doko-de bas-ni noremas-ka*
Is there a guide who speaks English?	英語のガイドがいますか。	*aygo-no gighd-ga imas-ka*
What trips can we take around the area?	どこか楽しい小旅行はありますか。	*doko-ka tanoshee shoh-ryokoh-wa arimas-ka*
Are there any excursions?	観光ツアーがありますか。	*kankoh-tsuah-ga arimas-ka*
Where do they go to?	どこへ行きますか。	*doko-e ikimas-ka*
We'd like to go to...	…へ行きたいんですが	*... e ikitigh-n des-nga*
How long is the trip?	ツアーは何時間かかりますか。	*tsuah-wa nan-jikan kakarimas-ka*
How long do we stay in...?	…にはどのくらい滞在しますか。	*... ni-wa dono kurigh tigh-zigh shimas-ka*
Are there any guided tours?	ガイド付きツアーがありますか。	*gighd-tski-tsua-ga arimas-ka*
How much free time will we have there?	どのぐらい自由時間がありますか。	*dono-gurigh jiyoo jikan-ga arimas-ka*
We want to go hiking	ハイキングに行きたいんです。	*highking-ni iki-tigh-n des-nga*
Can we hire a guide?	ガイドをたのめますか。	*gighd-o tanomemas-ka*
Can I book mountain huts?	山小屋が予約出来ますか。	*yama-goya-ga yoyaku dekimas-ka*
What time does...open?	何時に…が開きますか。	*nanji-ni ... ga akimas-ka*
What time does...close?	何時に…が閉まりますか。	*nanji-ni ... ga shimarimas-ka*
What days is...open?	何曜日に…が開いていますか。	*nanyohbi-ni ... ga igh-tay imas-ka*
What days is...closed?	何曜日に…が閉まっていますか。	*nanyohbi-ni ... ga shimat-tay imas-ka*
What's the admission price?	入場料はいくらですか。	*nyoojoh-ryoh-wa ikura des-ka*
Is there...	…の割引切符ありますか。	*... no waribiki kippu arimas-ka*
– a group discount?	グループ	*groop*
– a child discount?	子供	*kodomo*
– a discount for pensioners?	65歳以上	*rokujoo-go-sigh ijoh*
Can I take (flash) photos?	（フラッシュで）写真を撮ってもいいですか。	*(frash-de) shashin-o totte-mo ee des-ka*
Can I film here?	撮影してもいいですか。	*satsu-ay shtay-mo ee des-ka*
Do you have any postcards of...?	…の絵葉書がありますか。	*... no eha-gaki-ga arimas-ka*

Do you have an English...?	英語の…ありますか。 *aygo-no ... arimas-ka*
– catalogue?	カタログ *katarog*
– programme?	プログラム *program*
– brochure?	パンフレット *panfretto*

.2 Going out

Information about entertainment appears in the English language newspapers and in the visitors' guides which can be picked up in hotels. In Tokyo there is a Teletourist service which provides information about events and entertainment in English. Evening dress is rarely worn to the theatre. Shows open earlier than in Europe, usually 6.30 or 7.00. Traditional theatre includes *Kabuki*, *No* and *Bunraku*. Films generally are shown in the language of origin with Japanese subtitles.

Do you have this week's/month's entertainment guide?	今週／今月のプログラムありますか。 *konshoo / kongets-no program arimas-ka*
What's on tonight?	今晩のプログラムはどうですか。 *komban-no program-wa doh des-ka*
We want to go to...	…に行きたいんですが *... ni ikitigh-n des-nga*
Which films are showing?	どんな映画がありますか。 *donna ayga-ga arimas-ka*
What sort of film is that?	どのような映画ですか。 *dono yoh-na ayga des-ka*
rated adult (over 18)	成人映画 *sayjin ayga*
original version	オリジナル版 *orijinaru-ban*
subtitled	字幕付きで *jimaku-tski-de*
dubbed	吹替で *fuki-kae-de*
Is it a continuous showing?	繰り返し上演しますか。 *kuri-keashi joh-en shimas-ka*
What's on at...?	何かいい…はありますか。 *nani-ka ee ... wa arimas-ka*
– the theatre?	ショー *shoh*
– the concert hall?	音楽会 *ongak-kigh*
– the opera?	オペラ *opera*
Where can I find a good disco around here?	この辺にいいディスコはありますか。 *kono-hen-ni ee disko-wa arimas-ka*
Is it members only?	会員だけですか。 *kigh-in-dakay des-ka*
Where can I find a good nightclub around here?	この辺にいいナイト・クラブはありますか。 *kono-hen-ni ee night-krab-wa arimas-ka*

Is it evening wear only? ___	正装は必要ですか。
	saysoh-wa hits-yoh des-ka
What time does the _____ show start?	ショーは何時からですか。
	shoh-wa nanji-kara des-ka

11 .3 Booking tickets

Could you book...? _____	予約出来ますか。
	yoyaku dekimas-ka
– some tickets_____	切符
	kippu
– a seat in the stalls _____	一階席で
	ik-kigh-seki-de
– a seat on the balcony ____	二階席で
	ni-kigh-seki-de
– box seats _____	ボックス席で
	boks-seki-de
– a table at the front _____	前方で
	zempoh-de
– in the middle_____	中ごろで
	naka-goro-de
– at the back _____	後方で
	koh-hoh-de
Could I book...seats _____ for the...o'clock performance?	…時の上演の切符を…枚予約出来ますか。
	... ji-no joh-en-no kippu-o ... migh yoyaku deki-mas-ka
Are there any seats _____ left for tonight?	今晩の切符はまだありますか。
	komban-no kippu-wa mada arimas-ka
How much is a ticket? _____	一枚いくらですか。
	ichimigh ikura des-ka
When can I pick the _____ tickets up?	切符はいつもらえますか。
	kippu-wa its morae-mas-ka
I've got a reservation _____	予約しました。
	yoyaku shimashta
My name's... _____	私の名前は…です。
	watashi-no na-migh-wa ... des

どの上演に予約したいんですか。 _____	Which performance do you want to book for?
どんな座席がほしいんですか。 _____	Where would you like to sit?
すみませんが、売切れです。 _____	Everything's sold out
立ち見席だけ残っています。 _____	It's standing room only
二階席だけ残っています。 _____	We've only got balcony seats left
一階席だけ残っています。 _____	We've only got stalls seats left
前の座席が残っています。 _____	We've only got seats left at the front
後の座席が残っています。 _____	We've only got seats left at the back
何枚ですか。 _____	How many seats would you like?
…時までに切符を取りに来なければなり _____ ません。	You'll have to pick up the tickets before...o'clock
切符を見せて下さい。 _____	Tickets, please
こちらの席です。 _____	This is your seat

Sports

12 **S**ports

The most popular spectator sports are baseball, soccer and *sumo*. There are no public golf courses, but golf driving ranges are found in most places. Public tennis courts get very booked up. Fitness and sports clubs are widespread.

12 .1 **S**porting questions

Where can we... around here?	この辺で…が出来ますか。 *kono-hen-de ... ga dekimas-ka*
Is there a...around here?	この辺に…はありますか。 *kono-hen-ni ... wa arimas-ka*
Can I hire a...here?	ここで…が借りられますか。 *kook-de ... ga kari-rare-mas-ka*
Can I take...lessons?	…のレッスンが受けられますか。 *... no ressun-ga uke-rare-mas-ka*
How much is that per hour/per day/a turn?	一時間／一日／一回いくらですか。 *ichi-jikan/ichinichi/ik-kigh ikura des-ka*
Do I need a permit for that?	許可書が必要ですか。 *kyokasho-ga hits-yoh des-ka*
Where can I get the permit?	許可書はどこで発行されますか。 *kyokasho-wa doko-de hak-koh saremas-ka*

12 .2 **B**y the waterfront

Is it a long way to the sea still?	海岸までまだ遠いですか。 *kigh-gan maday mada toh-i des-ka*
Is there a...around here?	この辺に…はありますか。 *kono hen-ni ... wa arimas-ka*
– a swimming pool	プール *pooru*
– a sandy beach	砂浜 *sunahama*
– mooring	埠頭 *f-toh*
Are there any rocks here?	この辺には岩がありますか。 *kono-hen-ni-wa iwa-ga arimas-ka*
When's high/low tide?	いつ満潮／干潮ですか。 *its manchoh/kanchoh des-ka*
What's the water temperature?	水温は何度ですか。 *swee-on-wa nando des-ka*
Is it (very) deep here?	（とても）深いですか。 *(totemo) fu-kigh des-ka*
Can you stand here?	立てますか。 *tatemas-ka*
Is it safe (for children) to swim here?	（子供が）安全に泳げますか。 *(kodomo-ga) anzen-ni oyogemas-ka*
Are there any currents?	流れはきついですか。 *nagare-wa kitsui des-ka*

Are there any rapids/	この川に急流／滝がありますか。
waterfalls in this river?	*kono kawa-ni kyooryoo/taki-ga arimas-ka*
What does that flag/	あの旗／ブイはどういう意味ですか。
buoy mean?	*ano hata/bui-wa doh yoo imi des-ka*

つり場	要許可書	サーフィン禁止
Fishing water	Permits only	No surfing
危険／注意	遊泳禁止	つり禁止
Danger	No swimming	No fishing

12 .3 In the snow

Can I take ski lessons	ここでスキーのレッスンが受けられますか。
here?	*koko-de skee-ga naraemas-ka*
for beginners/advanced	初心者／上級
	shoshinsha / joh-kyoo
How large are the	グループは何人ぐらいですか。
groups?	*groop-wa nannin-gurigh des-ka*
What language are	何語で教えられますか。
the classes in?	*nanigo-de oshie-raremas-ka*
I'd like a lift pass,	リフトの一日券を下さい。
please	*rift-no ichinichi-ken-o kuda-sigh*
Must I give you a	写真がいりますか。
passport photo?	*shashin-ga irimas-ka*
Where can I have a	どこで写真を撮ってもらえますか。
passport photo taken?	*doko-de shashin-o tottay moraemas-ka*
Where are the	初心者のゲレンデはどこですか。
beginners' slopes?	*shoshinsha no gerenday-wa doko des-ka*
Are there any runs	この辺でクロスカントリースキーが
for cross-country skiing?	できますか。
	kono hen-de kros-kantree-skee-ga dekimas- ka
Are the...in operation?	…は動いていますか。
	... wa ugoitay-imas-ka
– ski lifts	スキーリフト
	skeerift
– chair lifts	リフト
	rift
Are the slopes usable?	ゲレンデは滑降可能ですか。
	gerenday-wa kakkoh kanoh des-ka

Sports

12

Sickness

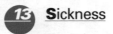

13 Sickness

English speaking hospitals or clinics can be found in most large cities. Because of the high cost of medical and dental treatment, insurance is advised when travelling. There are pharmacies in every neighbourhood and they are easily found.

13 .1 Call (fetch) the doctor

Could you call/fetch a _____ doctor quickly, please?
早くお医者さんを呼んで／連れてきて下さい。
hayaku o-isha-san-o yonded/tsretay-kitaykuda-sigh

When does the doctor _____ have surgery?
お医者さんの診察時間はいつですか。
o-isha-san-no shinsats- jikan-wa its des-ka

When can the doctor _____ come?
お医者さんはいつ来れますか。
o-isha-san-wa its koremas-ka

I'd like to make an _____ appointment to see the doctor
お医者さんの予約をして下さい。
o-isha-san-no yoyaku-o shtay kuda-sigh

I've got an appointment _____ to see the doctor at...
私は…時にお医者さんに会う約束があります。
watashi-wa ... ji-ni o-isha-san-ni au yakusoku-ga arimas

Which doctor (chemist) has night/weekend duty?
どの医者（薬局）が夜勤／週末勤務ですか。
dono isha (yak-kyoku)-ga yakin/shoomats kimmu des-ka

13 .2 Patient's ailments

I don't feel well _____
具合が悪いんです。
gu-igh-ga waru-i-n des

I'm dizzy _____
めまいがします。
me-migh-ga shimas

– ill _____
病気です。
byohki des

– sick _____
気分が悪いんです。
kibun-ga waru-i-n des

I've got a cold _____
風邪です。
kazay des

It hurts here _____
ここが痛いんです。
koko-ga i-tigh-n des

I've been throwing up _____
もどしてしまったんです。
modoshtay shimatta-n des

I'm running a _____ temperature of...degrees
…度の熱があります。
... do-no nets-ga arimas

I've been stung _____
…に刺されました。
... ni sasare-mashta

– by a hornet _____
スズメバチ
suzume-bachi

– by an insect _____
虫
mushi

Sickness

– by a jellyfish	クラゲ *kuragay*
I've been bitten	…に噛まれました。 *... ni kamare-mashta*
– by a dog	犬 *inu*
– by a snake	蛇 *hebi*
– by an animal	動物 *dohbuts*
I've cut myself	切り傷をつけました。 *kiri-kizu-o tskemashta*
I've burned myself	やけどをしました。 *yakedo-o shimashta*
I've grazed myself	肌をすりむきました。 *hada-o suri-muki-mashta*
I've had a fall	ころびました。 *korobimashta*
I've sprained my ankle	足首をくじきました。 *ashi-kubi-o kujikimashta*

.3 The consultation

症状は何ですか。	What seems to be the problem?
この症状はどのぐらい続いていますか。	How long have you had these symptoms?
この症状は初めてですか。	Have you had this trouble before?
熱は何度ですか。	How high is your temperature?
脱いで下さい。	Get undressed, please
上着を取って下さい。	Strip to the waist, please
あそこで脱いでください。	You can undress there
左/右腕をまくって下さい。	Roll up your left/right sleeve, please
ここに横になって下さい。	Lie down here, please
ここが痛いですか。	Does this hurt?
深呼吸してください。	Breathe deeply
口を開けて下さい。	Open your mouth

Patient's medical history

I'm a diabetic	糖尿病です。 *toh-nyoh-byoh des*
I have a heart condition	心臓病です。 *shinzoh-byoh des*
I have asthma	喘息病です。 *shinzoh-byoh des*

Sickness

13

97

I'm allergic to... ___	…に対してアレルギーです。
	... ni tigh-shtay arerugee des
I'm...months pregnant ___	…何ヶ月の妊娠です。
	... kagetsu-no ninshin des
I'm on a diet ___	食事制限をしています。
	shokuji saygen-o shtay imas
I'm on medication/ ___ the pill	薬／ピルを使っています。
	kusuri/piru-o tskattay imas
I've had a heart attack ___ once before	心臓麻痺をおこしたことがあります。
	shinzoh mahi-o okoshta koto-ga arimas
I've had a(n)...operation ___	…の手術を受けました。
	... no shujuts-o ukemashta
I've been ill recently ___	最近まで病気でした。
	sigh-kin maday byohki deshta
I've got an ulcer ___	潰瘍があります。
	kigh-yoh-ga arimas
I've got my period ___	月経です。
	gek-kay des

何かに対してアレルギーがありますか。 ___	Do you have any allergies?
薬を使っていますか。 ___	Are you on any medication?
食事制限をしていますか。 ___	Are you on a diet?
妊娠中ですか。 ___	Are you pregnant?
破傷風の予防接種をしましたか。 ___	Have you had a tetanus injection?

The diagnosis

深刻なものではありません。 ___	It's nothing serious
…が骨折しています。 ___	Your...is broken
…にあざがあります。 ___	You've got a/some bruised...
…をくじいています。 ___	You've got (a) torn...
炎症を起こしています。 ___	You've got an inflammation
虫垂炎を起こしています。 ___	You've got appendicitis
気管支炎を起こしています。 ___	You've got bronchitis
性病です。 ___	You've got a venereal disease
流行性感冒です。 ___	You've got the flu
心臓麻痺でした。 ___	You've had a heart attack
（ビールス／バクテリアに） 感染しています。 ___	You've got an infection (viral.../bacterial...)
肺炎です。 ___	You've got pneumonia
潰瘍があります。 ___	You've got an ulcer
筋をひきちがえました。 ___	You've pulled a muscle
腟の感染症です。 ___	You've got a vaginal infection

Sickness

13

食中毒です。＿＿＿＿＿＿＿＿＿＿	You've got food poisoning
日射病です。＿＿＿＿＿＿＿＿＿＿	You've got sunstroke
…に対してアレルギーがあります。＿＿＿	You're allergic to...
妊娠です。＿＿＿＿＿＿＿＿＿＿＿	You're pregnant
あなたの血液／小便／糞便を＿＿＿＿ 検査したいんです。	I'd like to have your blood/urine/stools tested
傷口を縫い合わせなければなりません。＿＿	It needs stitching
専門医／病院に紹介します。＿＿＿＿＿	I'm referring you to a specialist/sending you to hospital
X線写真を撮らなければなりません。＿＿＿	You'll need to have some x-rays taken
ちょっと待合室で待っていて下さい。＿＿＿	Could you wait in the waiting room, please?
手術が必要です。＿＿＿＿＿＿＿＿	You'll need an operation

Is it contagious?＿＿＿＿＿	伝染性ですか。	densensay des-ka
How long do I have to stay...?	どのぐらい長く…にいなければなりませんか。	dono gu-righ nagaku ... ni inakareba nari-masen-ka
– in bed ＿＿＿＿＿＿＿	ベッド	beddo
– in hospital ＿＿＿＿＿	病院	byoh-in
Do I have to go on a special diet?	食事制限をしなければなりませんか。	shokuji saygen-o shinakereba narimasen-ka
Am I allowed to travel? ＿＿＿	旅行してもいいですか	ryokoh shtay-mo ee des-ka
When do I have to come back?	いつ伺わなければなりませんか。	its ukagawa-nakereba narimasen-ka
I'll come back tomorrow ＿＿	また明日伺います。	mata ashta uka-gigh-imas

---

明日／…日後にここにきて下さい。＿＿＿＿＿＿	Come back tomorrow/ in...days' time	

🔞 .4 Medication and prescriptions

How do I take this medicine?	この薬はどう飲みますか。	kono kusuri-wa doh nomimas-ka
How many capsules/ drops/injections/spoonfuls /tablets each time?	一回どのくらいずつですか。	ik-kigh dono-kurigh-zuts des-ka
How many times a day? ＿＿	一日何回ずつですか。	ichinichi nankigh-zuts des-ka
I've forgotten my medication. At home I take...	薬を忘れてしまったんですが、普段は…を使 っています。	kusuri-o wasurete-shimatta-n-des-nga, foodan-wa ... o tskattay imas
Could you make out a prescription for me?	処方を書いて下さいませんか。	shohoh-o kaitay kudasa-i-masen-ka

抗生物質／飲み薬／	_____	I'm prescribing
トランキライザー／		antibiotics/a mixture/a
鎮痛剤の処方を書きます。		tranquilliser/pain killers
休まなければなりません。	_____	Have lots of rest
外へ出かけてはいけません。	_____	Stay indoors
寝ていなければなりません。	_____	Stay in bed

食事前に	注射	錠剤
before meals	**injections**	**tablets**
カプセル	外用のみ	飲む
capsules	**not for internal use**	**take**
水に溶かす	軟膏	この薬は自動車の
dissolve in water	**ointment**	運転に影響を
ドロップ	つける	きたします。
drops	**rub on**	**this medication**
…時間おきに	スプーン（大／小）	**impairs your**
every...hours	**spoonfuls**	**driving**
完全に治療を終	**(tablespoons/teasp**	一日…回
わらせる	**oons)**	**...times a day**
finish the course	全部飲んで下さい	
…日間	**swallow whole**	
for...days		

13 .5 At the dentist's

Do you know a good _____ dentist?	いい歯医者を知っていますか。
	ee ha-isha-o shtay imas-ka
Could you make _____ a dentist's appointment for me? It's urgent	私のために歯医者に予約して下さいませんか。 急いでいます。
	watashi-no tame-ni ha-isha-ni yoyaku shtay kudasa-i-masen-ka. isoi-day imas
Can I come in today, _____ please?	今日伺えますか。
	kyoh uka-gigh-emas-ka
I have (terrible)_____ toothache	（すごく）歯が痛いんです。
	(sugoku) ha-ga i-tigh-n des
Could you prescribe/ _____ give me a painkiller?	鎮痛剤の処方を書いて下さい／鎮痛剤をくだ さい。
	chintsoo-zigh-no shohoh-o kaitay kuda-sigh/chintsoo-zigh-o kuda-sigh
A piece of my tooth _____ has broken off	歯がおれました。
	ha-ga oremashta
My filling's come out _____	歯につめたのがとれました。
	ha-ni tsumeta-no-ga toremashta
I've got a broken crown____	歯冠がこわれました。
	shikan-ga koware-mashta
I'd like a local _____ anaesthetic	局所麻酔をかけてください。
	kyokusho maswee-o kaketay kuda-sigh
I don't want a local _____ anaesthetic	局所麻酔をかけないでください。
	kyokusho maswee-o kake-nigh-de kuda-sigh

Sickness

13

Can you do a makeshift ___ repair job?	応急治療をしてください。
	ohkyoo chiryo-o shtay kuda-sigh
I don't want this tooth ___ pulled	この歯は抜かないでください。
	kono ha-wa nuka-nigh-de kuda-sigh
My dentures are _____ broken. Can you fix them?	入れ歯がこわれましたが、修理できますか。
	ireba-ga kowaremashta-ga, shoori dekimas-ka

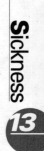

どの歯が痛いんですか。_____	Which tooth hurts?
はれています。_____	You've got an abscess
歯茎の治療が必要です。_____	I'll have to do a root canal
局所麻酔をかけます。_____	I'm giving you a local anaesthetic
この歯をつめなければ／抜かなければ／ ___ けずらなければなりません。	I'll have to fill/pull this tooth/file this...down
穴を開けなければなりません。_____	I'll have to drill
口を大きく開けて下さい。_____	Open wide, please
口を閉めて下さい。_____	Close your mouth, please
口をゆすいで下さい。_____	Rinse, please
まだ痛いですか。_____	Does it hurt still?

In trouble

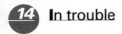

14 In trouble

Emergency phone numbers: Police: 110; Ambulance/Fire: 119. On a public phone, press the red button and dial; no money is necessary. Speak slowly and clearly if there is no Japanese speaker with you. If you are in difficulty you can ring the Travel Phone service and speak to someone in English; insert 10 yen and dial 106 and in English say to the operator 'Collect call TIC'. The coin will be returned.

14 .1 Asking for help

Help!	助けて！
	tas-ketay!
Fire!	火事！
	kaji!
Police!	警察！
	kay-sats!
Quick!	早く！
	hayaku!
Danger!	危ない！
	abu-nigh!
Watch out!/Be careful!	あぶない！
	abu-nigh!
Stop!	止まれ！
	tomaray!
Don't!	しないで！／するな！
	shi-nigh-de!/suru-na!
Let go!	手をどけてよ！／手をはなして！
	te-o doketay yo!/te-o hanashtay!
Stop that thief!	泥棒を止めて！
	doroboh-o tometay!
Could you help me, please?	助けて下さい。
	tas-ketay kuda-sigh
Where's the police station/emergency exit/fire escape?	警察署／非常口／避難階段はどこですか。
	kaysats-sho/hijoh-guchi/hinan-kigh-dan-wa doko des-ka
Where's the fire extinguisher?	消火器はどこですか。
	shohkaki-wa doko-des-ka
Call the fire brigade!	消防車を呼んで！
	shohbohsha-o yonday!
Call the police!	警察を呼んで！
	kaysats-o yonday!
Call an ambulance!	救急車を呼んで！
	kyookyoosha-o yonday!
Where's the nearest phone?	電話はどこですか。
	denwa-wa doko des-ka
Could I use your phone?	電話を使わせてください。
	denwa-o ts-kawashtay kuda-sigh
What's the number for the police?	警察は何番ですか。
	kay-sats-wa namban des-ka

In trouble

14

🔢 .2 Loss

The railways, underground lines and taxi companies have lost-and-found services.

I've lost my purse/wallet	財布をなくしました。 *sighfu-o naku-shimashta*
I left my...yesterday	昨日…を置き忘れました。 *kinoh ... o okiwasure-mashta*
I left my...here	ここに…を置き忘れました。 *koko-ni ... o oki-wasure-mashta*
Did you find my...?	私の…が見つかりましたか。 *watashi-no ... ga mitsukari-mashta-ka*
It was right here	ここにありました。 *koko-ni arimashta*
It's quite valuable	とても貴重品です。 *totemo kichoh-hin des*
Where's the lost property office?	忘れ物係りはどこですか。 *wasuremono-kakari-wa doko des-ka*

🔢 .3 Accidents

Robbery and violent crime are rare in Japan. The police maintain a visible presence through a network of small police stations called *koban*, usually found near railway stations. The policemen will help you find an address.

There's been an accident	事故が起きました。 *jiko-ga okimashta*
Someone's fallen into the water	人が水に落ちました。 *shto-ga mizu-ni ochimashta*
There's a fire	火事です。 *kaji des*
Is anyone hurt?	怪我をした人いますか。 *kega-o shita shto imas-ka*
Some people have been injured	怪我人がいます。 *keganin-ga imas*
No one's been injured	怪我人はいません。 *keganin-wa imasen*
There's someone in the car/train still	人がまだ車／列車に残っています。 *shto-ga mada kuruma/ressha-ni nokottay imas*
It's not too bad. Don't worry	それほどでもありません。心配しないで下さい。 *sore-hodo demo arimasen. shimpigh shi-nigh-de kuda-sigh*
Leave everything the way it is, please	何もさわらないで下さい。 *nani-mo sawara-nigh-de kuda-sigh*
I want to talk to the police first	まず警察と話したいんです。 *mazu kaysats-to hanashi-tigh-n des*
I want to take a photo first	まず写真を取りたいんです。 *mazu shashin-o tori-tigh-n des*
Here's my name and address	これが私の名前と住所です。 *kore-ga watashi-no na-migh-to joosho des*

Could I have your _____ name and address?	あなたの名前と住所を教えて下さい。 *anata-no na-migh-to joosho-o oshietay kuda-sigh*
Could I see some _____ identification/your insurance papers?	身分証明書／保険証書を見せて下さい。 *mibun shohmaysho/hokan-shohsho-o misetay kuda-sigh*
Will you act as a _____ witness?	証人になってくれますか。 *shohnin-ni nattay kuremas-ka*
I need the details _____ for the insurance	保険のために詳細が必要です。 *hoken-no tame-ni shoh-sigh-ga hits-yoh des*
Are you insured? _____	保険に入っていますか。 *hoken-ni hight-tay imas-ka*
Could you sign here, _____ please?	ここにサインをして下さい。 *koko-ni sign-o shtay kuda-sigh*

14.4 Theft

I've been robbed _____	盗まれました。 *nusu-mare-mashta*
My...has been stolen _____	…が盗まれました。 *... ga nusu-mare-mashta*

14.5 Missing person

I've lost my child/ _____ grandmother	子供／祖母が迷子になりました。 *kodomo/sobo-ga mighgo-ni narimashta*
Could you help me _____ find him/her?	捜すのを手伝って下さい。 *sagasu-no-o tetsudattay kuda-sigh*
Have you seen a _____ small child?	小さい子を見ましたか。 *chee-sigh ko-o mimashta-ka*
He's/she's...years old _____	…歳です。 *... sigh des*
He's/she's got short/ _____ long/blond/red/brown/black/grey/curly/ straight/frizzy hair	髪が短い／長い／金髪／赤い／茶色／黒い／白髪／巻き毛／真っ直ぐ／縮れ毛です。 *kami-ga miji-kigh/na-gigh/kimpats/a-kigh/cha-iro/kuro-i/hakuhats/maki-ge/mas-sugu/chijirege des*
with a ponytail _____	ポニーテールで *ponee-tehru des*
with plaits _____	三つ編みで *mitsu-ami-de*
in a bun _____	たばねて *tabanetay*
He's/she's got blue/ _____ brown eyes	目が青い…茶色です。 *me-ga ao-i ... cha-iro des*
He's wearing _____ swimming trunks	海水パンツをはいています。 *kigh-swee pants-o high-tay imas*
...mountaineering boots ___	登山靴をはいています。 *tohzan-gutsu-o high-tay imas*
with glasses _____	眼鏡をかけています。 *meganay-o kaketay imas*
tall/short_____	大きい／小さい *oh-kee/chee-sigh*
This is a photo of _____ him/her	彼…彼女の写真です。 *kare ... kanoji-no shashin des*

In trouble

14

An arrest

運転免許証を見せて下さい。 _____	Your driving licence, please
スピード違反です。 _____	You were speeding
ここは駐車禁止です。 _____	You're not allowed to park here
ライトがついていません。 _____	Your lights aren't working
罰金は…円です。 _____	That's a...yen fine
今払いますか。 _____	Do you want to pay on the spot?
今払わなければなりません。 _____	You'll have to pay on the spot

I don't speak _____ Japanese	日本語が話せません。
	nihongo-ga hanase-masen
I didn't see the sign _____	あの交通標識が見えませんでした。
	ano kohtsoo-hyohshiki-ga miemasen deshta
I don't understand _____ what it says	あの標識は分かりません。
	ano hyohshiki-wa wakarimasen
I was only doing... _____ kilometres an hour	時速…キロだけで走っていました。
	jisoku ...kiro-dake-de hashittay imashta
I'll have my car _____ checked	車を検査してもらいます。
	kuruma-o kensa shte-morigh-mas
I was blinded by _____ oncoming lights	対向車のライトに目がくらみました。
	tigh-koh-sha-no righto-ni me-ga kurami-mashta

At the police station

どこで起こりましたか。 _____	Where did it happen?
何をなくしましたか。 _____	What's missing?
何が盗まれましたか。 _____	What's been taken?
身分証明書を見せて下さい。 _____	Could I see some identification?
それは何時でしたか。 _____	What time did it happen?
誰が関係しましたか。 _____	Who was involved?
証人がいますか。 _____	Are there any witnesses?
ここに記入してください。 _____	Fill this out, please
ここにサインをして下さい。 _____	Sign here, please
通訳が必要ですか。 _____	Do you want an interpreter?

In trouble

14

I want to report a _____ collision/missing person/rape	衝突／まい子／強姦を届けに来ました。
	shohtots/mighgo/gohkan-o todoke-ni kimashta
Could you make out a _____ report, please?	調書を書いて下さい。
	chohsho-o kigh-tay kuda-sigh
Could I have a copy _____ for the insurance?	保険のために写しをください。
	hoken-no tame-ni utsushi-o kuda-sigh
I've lost everything _____	全部失いました。
	zembu ushi-nigh-mashta
I've lost all my money ____	お金が全部なくなりました。
	okane-ga zenbu nakunari-mashta
Could you lend me _____ some money?	お金を少し貸して下さいますか。
	okane-o skoshi kashtay kuda-sigh-mas-ka
I'd like an interpreter _____	通訳が必要です。
	tsooyaku-ga hits-yoh des
I'm innocent _____	私は無罪です。
	watashi-wa muzigh des
I don't know anything ____ about it	何も知りません。
	nan-ni-mo shirimasen
I want to speak to _____ someone	…の人と話したいんです。
	... no shto-to hanashi-tigh-n des
...from the British _____ consulate	イギリス領事館
	igirisu ryohjikan
...from the British _____ embassy	イギリス大使館
	igirisu tigh-shikan
I want a lawyer who _____ speaks English	英語が話せる弁護士がほしいんです。
	eigo ga hanaseru bengoshi-ga hoshee-n des

In trouble

14

107

15

Word list

Word list English - Japanese

The following word list is meant to supplement the chapters in this book. Where the meaning of the word is very broad, notes have been inserted to show the sense in which the Japanese word is used. Some of the words not contained in this list can be found elsewhere in the book, e.g. alongside the diagrams of the car, bicycle and camping equipment.

A

100 grams	100グラム	hyaku-gram
a little	少し	skosh
about	約／だいたい	yaku/digh-tigh
above	上	ue
abroad	外国	gigh-kok
abundant	豊富な	hohfu-na
accident	事故	jiko
adder	マムシ	mamushi
addition	計算	kaysan
address	住所	joo-sho
admission	入場	nyoojoh
admission price	入場料	nyoojoh-ryoh
advice	忠告	choo-kok
after	…の後で	... no ato-de
afternoon	午後	gogo
aftershave	アフターシェーブローション	aftah-shayb rohshon
again	もう一度	moh ichido
against	…に対して	... ni tigh-shtay
age	年齢	nen-ray
Aids	エイズ	ayz
air conditioning	エアコン	e-a-kon
air mattress	エア・マットレス	e-a mattoresu
aircraft	飛行機	hikohki
airport	空港	kookoh
alarm	警告	kay-kok
alarm clock	目覚まし時計	mezamashi-dokay
alcohol	アルコール	aru-kohru
all the time	ずっと	zutto
allergic	アレルギー	areru-gee
alone	一人で	shtori day
always	いつも	its-mo
ambulance	救急車	kyoo-kyoo-sha
amount	総額	soh-gak
amusement park	遊園地	yoo-en-chi
anaesthetize (local)	局所麻酔をかける	kyokusho-maswee-o kakeru
anchovy	アンチョビー	anchobee
angry	おこった	okotta
animal	動物	doh-buts
ankle	くるぶし	kurubushi
answer	答え／返事	ko-tigh/henji
ant	アリ	ari
antibiotics	抗生物質	kohsay busshits
antifreeze	不凍液	f-toh-eki
antique	古代の	kodigh-no
antiques	古美術／骨董品	kobijuts/kottoh-hin

anus	肛門	*kohmon*
apartment	アパート	*a-pahto*
aperitif	食前酒	*shokuzen-shu*
apologies	許し	*yurushi*
apple	リンゴ	*ringo*
apple juice	リンゴジュース	*ringo joos*
apple pie	アップルパイ	*appuru pigh*
apple sauce	アップルソース	*appuru sohsu*
appointment	約束	*yak-soku*
apricot	アンズ	*anzu*
April	四月	*shigats*
architecture	建築	*ken-chiku*
area	環境	*kankyoh*
arm	腕	*uday*
arrange	約束する	*yak-soku suru*
arrive	着く	*tsuku*
arrow	矢印	*ya-jirushi*
art	芸術	*gay-juts*
artery	動脈	*doh-myaku*
article	物	*mono*
artificial respiration	人口呼吸	*jinkoh kokyoo*
ashtray	灰皿	*high-zara*
ask	尋ねる／問う	*tazuneru/tou*
ask (for)	頼む	*tanomu*
asparagus	アスパラガス	*asparagas*
aspirin	アスピリン	*aspirin*
assault	強姦	*gohkan*
at home	家に	*uchi-ni*
at night	夜	*yoru*
at the back	後に	*ushiro-ni*
at the front	前に	*ma-e-ni*
at the latest	遅くても	*osokutemo*
aubergine	ナス	*nas*
August	八月	*hachi-gats*
automatic	自動的	*jodoh-teki*
autumn	秋	*aki*
avalanche	雪崩	*nadaray*
awake	起きた	*okita*
awning	日よけ	*hiyokay*

B

baby	赤ちゃん	*aka-chan*
baby sitter	ベビーシッター	*baybee-shittah*
back	背中	*senaka*
backpack	リュックサック	*ryukkusakku*
bacon	ベーコン	*behkon*
bad	悪い	*waru-i*
bad (terrible)	ひどい／大変	*hidoi/tigh-hen*
bag	カバン	*kaban*
baker	パン屋	*pan-ya*
balcony	バルコニー	*barukonee*
ball	ボール／球	*bohru/tama*
ballet	バレー	*baray*
ballpoint pen	ボールペン	*bohru-pen*
banana	バナナ	*banana*
bandage	包帯	*hoh-tigh*
bank	銀行	*gin-koh*

bank (river)	岸	*kishi*
bar (cafe)	バー	*bah*
bar (drinks' cabinet)	バー	*bah*
barbecue	バーベキュー	*bahbekyoo*
basketball (to play)	バスケットボール	*basketto-bohru*
bath	風呂／バス	*furo/bas*
bath towel	バスタオル	*bas-taoru*
bathing cap	海水帽	*kigh-swee boh*
bathing suit	水着	*mizu-gi*
bathroom	風呂場／バスルーム	*furoba/bas-room*
battery	バッテリー／電池	*betteree/denchi*
beach	浜／ビーチ	*hama/beechi*
beans	豆	*mamay*
beautiful	すばらしい／華美な	*subara-shee/kabi-na*
beautiful	美しい／きれいな	*utsuku-shee/kiray-na*
beauty parlour	美容院	*biyoh-in*
bed	ベッド／寝台	*beddo/shin-digh*
bee	ミツバチ	*mitsu-bachi*
beef	牛肉	*gyooniku*
beer	ビール	*beeru*
begin	始まる	*haji-maru*
beginner	初心者	*sho-shin-sha*
behind	後	*ushiro*
belt	ベルト	*beruto*
berth	寝台	*shin-digh*
better (to get)	元気になる／快復する	*genki-ni naru/kigh-fuku suru*
bicarb	重炭酸ソーダ	*jootan-san sohda*
bicycle	自転車	*jitensha*
bicycle pump	空気入れ	*kooki-iray*
bicycle repairman	自転車屋	*jitensha-ya*
bikini	ビキニ	*bikini*
bill	勘定	*kanjoh*
billiards (to play)	玉突きをする	*tama-tski-o suru*
birthday	誕生日	*tanjoh-bi*
biscuit	ビスケット／クッキー	*bisketto/kukkee*
bite	かむ	*kamu*
bitter	苦い	*ni-gigh*
black	黒い	*kuro-i*
bland (taste)	味のない	*aji-no nigh*
blanket	毛布	*mohf*
bleach	漂白する／脱色する	*hyoh-hak suru/dasshok suru*
blister	水膨れ	*mizu-buku-ray*
blond	金髪	*kimpats*
blood	血液	*kets-eki*
blood pressure	血圧	*kets-ats*
bloody nose	鼻血	*hana-ji*
blouse	ブラウス	*burausu*
blow dry	ブロー・ドライ	*buroh-drigh*
blue	青い	*a-oi*
blunt	鈍い	*nibui*
boat	ボート	*bohto*
body	体	*karada*
body milk	ボディーミルク	*bodee miru-k*
boiled	茹でた	*yudeta*
boiled ham	ハム	*hamu*

bonbon	ボンボン	bonbon
bone	骨	honay
bonnet	ボンネット	bon-netto
book	本	hon
book (verb)	予約する	yoyaku suru
booked (theatre ticket)	予約した	yoyaku shta
booking office (theatre ticket)	プレーガイド	pureh-gighdo
booking office (train)	みどりの窓口	midori-no mado-guchi
bookshop	本屋	hon-ya
border	国境	kokkyoh
bored (to be)	飽きた	akita
boring	面白くない／つまらない	omoshi-roku-nigh/tsumara-nigh
born	生まれた	umareta
borrow (from)	…から借りる	... kara kariru
botanical gardens	植物園	shokubutsu-en
both	両方	ryoh-hoh
bottle	びん	bin
bottle (baby's)	哺乳びん	honyoo-bin
bottle-warmer	哺乳びん保温器	honyoo-bin ho-onki
box	箱	hako
box (in theatre)	ボックス席で	bokks-seki-de
boy	男の子	otoko-no ko
bra	ブラジャー	burajah
bracelet	腕輪／ブレスレット	uday-wa/bures-retto
braised	煮込んだ	nikonda
brake	ブレーキ	brayki
brake oil	ブレーキオイル	brayki-oiru
bread	パン	pan
break	折る	oru
breakfast	朝ご飯	asa-gohan
breast	胸	munay
bridge	橋	hashi
briefs	パンツ／パンティー	pants/pantee
bring	持ってくる	mottay kuru
brochure	パンフレット	panfretto
broken	破れた／こわれた	yabureta/kowareta
brother (older, other's)	お兄さん	o-nee-san
brother (older, own)	兄	ani
brother (younger, other's)	弟さん	o-tohto-san
brother (younger, own)	弟	o-tohto
brown	茶色	cha-iro
bruise	あざができる	aza-ga dekiru
brush	ブラシ	burashi
Brussels sprouts	芽キャベツ	me-kyabets
bucket	バケツ	baketsu
bugs	害虫／ばい菌	gigh-choo/bigh-kin
building	建物	tate-mono
bun	菓子パン	kashi-pan
buoy	ブイ	bui
burglary	押し込み	oshikomi
burn	火傷	yakedo
burn (verb)	やける	yakeru
burnt	焼いた	yigh-ta
bus	バス	bas
bus station	バスの発着所	bas-no hachaku-jo

bus stop	バス停	*bas-tay*
business class	ビジネスクラス	*bijinesu-kuras*
business trip	出張	*shutchoh*
busy (schedule)	忙しい	*isogashee*
busy (traffic)	混雑	*konzats*
butane camping gas	ブタン・ガス	*butan-gas*
butcher	肉屋	*niku-ya*
butter	バター	*batah*
button	ボタン	*botan*
buy	買う	*ka-u*
by airmail	航空便で	*kohkoobin-de*
by phone	電話で	*denwa-de*

c

cabbage	キャベツ	*kyabets*
cabin	船室	*sen-shits*
cake	ケーキ	*kehki*
cake shop	ケーキ屋／お菓子屋	*kayki-ya/okashi-ya*
call	呼び出し	*yobi-dashi*
call (phone)	電話をする	*denwa-o suru*
called, to be	…と言う／…と言います	*... to yoo/... to eemas*
camera	カメラ	*kamera*
camp (verb)	キャンプする	*kyampu suru*
camp shop	キャンプ場売店	*kyampu-jo bigh-ten*
camp site	キャンプ場	*kyampu-jo*
camper	キャンピングカー	*kyamping-kah*
campfire	キャンプファイヤー	*kyampu-figh-yah*
camping guide	キャンプ案内	*kyampu an-nigh*
camping permit	キャンプ場使用許可書	*kyampu-jo shiyoh kyoka-sho*
cancel	取り消す	*tori-kes*
candle	ローソク	*rohsok*
canoe	カヌー	*ka-noo*
canoe (verb)	カヌーをこいで行く	*ka-noo-o ko-iday iku*
car	車／自動車	*kuruma/jidoh-sha*
car deck	自動車用の甲板	*jidoh-sha-yohno kampan*
car documents	車の証明書	*kuruma-no shohmay-sho*
car seat (child's)	ベビーシート	*bebee sheeto*
car trouble	車の故障	*kuruma-no koshoh*
caravan	キャラバン	*kyaraban*
cardigan	カーディガン	*kahdigan*
careful	注意深い	*choo-i-bu-kigh*
carrot	にんじん	*ninjin*
cartridge	カセットフィルム	*kasetto-firum*
cascade	滝	*taki*
cash desk	支払い所	*shi-harigh-jo*
casino	カジノ	*kajino*
cassette	カセット・テープ	*kasetto-tayp*
castle	城	*shiro*
cat	猫	*neko*
catalogue	カタログ	*katarog*
cathedral	大聖堂	*digh-say-doh*
cauliflower	カリフラワー	*kari-fura-wah*
cave	ほら穴	*hora-ana*

CD	シーディー	shee-dee
celebrate	祝う	iwau
cellotape	セロテープ	serotehpu
cemetery	墓地	bochi
centimetre	センチ（メートル）	senchi (mehtoru)
central heating	セントラル・ヒーティング	sentoraru-heetingu
centre	…の中の	... no naka-no
centre (city)	中心地	choo-shin-chi
chair	椅子	isu
chambermaid	ルーム係り	room-gakari
champagne	シャンペン	shanpen
change	変える	kaeru
change (money)	両替	ryoh-gigh
change (money) (verb)	両替する	ryoh-gigh suru
change (trains)	乗り換える	nori-ka-eru
change the baby's nappy	おむつを取り替える	omutsu-o tori-ka-eru
change the oil	オイルを交換する	oiru-o kohkan suru
charter flight	チャーター便	chahtah-bin
chat up	言い寄る	ee-yoru
cheers	乾杯	kam-pigh
cheese	チーズ	cheez
chef	コックさん	kukku-san
chemist	薬局	yakkyoku
cheque	小切手	kogit-tay
cherries	チェリー／サクランボ	cheree/sakurambo
chess (to play)	チェスをする	chesu-o suru
chewing gum	チューインガム	chooing-gam
chicken	ニワトリ	niwatori
child (other's)	お子さん	okosan
child (own)	子供	kodomo
child's seat	子供用いす	kodomo-yoh isu
chilled	冷たくした	tsumetaku shta
chin	あご	ago
chips	フライドポテト	frighdo poteto
chocolate	チョコレート	choko-rehto
choose	選択する／選ぶ	sentaku suru/erabu
chop (with breadcrumb)	カツレツ	katsuretsu
christian name	名前	na-migh
church	教会	kyoh-kigh
church service	礼拝	ray-high
cigar	葉巻	hamaki
cigar shop	たばこ屋	tabakoya
cigarette	たばこ	tabako
circle	円	en
circus	サーカス	sahkas
city	市	shi
clean	清潔な	sayketsu-na
clean (verb)	掃除する	sohji suru
clear	はっきりした	hakkiri shta
clearance (sale)	セール	sayru
clock	時計	to-kay
closed	閉まっている	shmatte-iru
closed off (road)	通行止め	tsoo-koh domay
clothes	衣服	if-ku
clothes hanger	ハンガー／衣紋掛け	han-gah/emon-kakay
clothes peg	洗濯ばさみ	sentaku-basami

clothing	衣類	i-rui
coach	リムジンバス	rimujin bas
coat	コート	kohto
cockroach	ゴキブリ／ アブラムシ	gokiburi/abura-mushi
cocoa	ココア	koko-a
cod	タラ	tara
coffee	コーヒー	koh-hee
coffee filter	コーヒー・ フィルター	koh-hee firutah
cognac	コニャック	konnyakku
cold	風邪	kazay
cold (not hot)	寒い	samu-i
collarbone	鎖骨	sakots
colleague	同僚	doh-ryoh
collision	衝突	shoh-tots
cologne	化粧水	keshoh-swee
colour	色	iro
colour pencils	色鉛筆	iro-empits
colour television	カラーテレビ	karah-terebi
colouring book	ぬり絵の本	nuri-e-no hon
comb	くし	kushi
come	来る	kuru
come back	戻って来る	modottay kuru
compartment	コンパートメント	konpahtomento
complaint	苦情	kujoh
complaint (illness)	痛み	itami
completely	全く	mattaku
compliment	賛辞	sanji
compulsory	義務	gimu
concert (classical)	コンサート	konsahto
concert hall	コンサートホール	konsahto-hohru
concussion	脳しんとう	noh-shintoh
condensed milk	クリーム	kureem
condom	コンドーム	kondohm
congratulate	祝う	iwa-u
connection	接続	setsu-zoku
constipation	便秘	bempi
consulate	領事館	ryohji-kan
consultation (house call by doctor)	往診	ohshin
contact lens	コンタクトレンズ	kontakuto-renzu
contagious	伝染性の	densensay-no
contraceptive	避妊の	hinin-no
contraceptive pill	避妊薬／ピル	hinin-yak/piru
cook	コック	kokku
cook (verb)	料理する	ryohri suru
copper	銅	doh
copy	コピー	kopee
corkscrew	コルク栓抜き	koruk-sen-nuki
corn flour	コーンスターチ	kohn-stahchi
corner	隅／角	sumi/kado
correct	正しい	tada-shee
correspond	文通する	bun-tsoo suru
corridor	廊下	rohka
costume	衣装	i-shoh
cot	ベビーベッド	bebee-beddo

cotton	木綿	momen
cotton wool	脱脂綿／綿	dasshi-men/wata
cough	咳	seki
cough (verb)	咳込む	seki-komu
cough mixture	咳止めシロップ	seki-domay shiroppu
counter	受付け	uke-tskay
country (nation)	国	kuni
country (rural area)	田舎	inaka
country code	国番号	kuni ban-go
courgette	ズッキーニ	zukkeenee
course (of treatment)	治療	chi-ryoh
cousin	いとこ	itoko
crab	蟹	kani
cream	クリーム	kureem
cream (fresh)	生クリーム	nama-kureemu
credit card	クレジット・カード	kurejitto-kahdo
crisps	ポテトチップ	poteto-chippu
croissant	クロワッサン	kuro-wasson
cross the road	横断する	ohdan suru
cross-country run	クロスカントリー スキー用のコース	kuros-kantoree-skee-yoh no kohs
cross-country skiing	クロスカントリー スキー	kuros-kantoree-skee
cross-country skis	クロスカントリー用 スキー	kuros-kantoreeyoh-skee
cry	泣く	naku
cubic metre	立方メートル	rippoh mehtoru
cucumber	キュウリ	kyoori
cuddly toy	ぬいぐるみ	nui-gurumi
cuff links	カフス・ボタン	kafs-botan
culottes	キュロット	kyoo-rotto
cup	茶わん	chawan
curly	巻き毛の	maki-ge-no
current	流れ／電流	nagaray/denryuh
cushion	クッション	kusshon
customary	普通／いつも	futsoo/itsumo
customs	税関	zaykan
cut	切る	kiru
cutlery	ナイフとフォークと スプーン	nighf-to fohk-to spoon
cycling	サイクリング	sigh-kuringu

D

dairy products	乳製品	nyoo-say-hin
damage	損害	son-gigh
dance	踊る	odoru
dandruff	ふけ	f-kay
danger	危険	kiken
dangerous	危険な	kiken-na
dark	暗い	ku-righ
date	デート	dayto
daughter (other's)	娘さん	musu-may-san
daughter (own)	娘	musu-may
day	日	hi
day (the whole)	まる一日	maru ichinichi
day before yesterday	一昨日	ototoi
dead	亡くなった	nakunatta

decaffeinated	カフェインなし／カフェインフリー	*kafayn-nashi/kafayn-free*
December	十二月	*joo-ni-gats*
deck chair	ビーチ・チェアー	*beechi-cheyah*
declare (customs)	申告する	*shin-koku suru*
deep	深い	*fu-kigh*
deep sea diving	スキンダイビング	*skin-dighbingu*
deepfreeze	冷凍庫	*raytohko*
degrees	度	*do*
delay	停滞／遅延	*tay-tigh/chi-en*
delicious	おいしい	*o-ishee*
dentist	歯医者	*ha-isha*
dentures	入れ歯	*ireba*
deodorant	デオドラント	*deodoranto*
department	部	*bu*
department store	デパート	*depahto*
departure	出発	*shuppats*
departure time	出発時間	*shuppats jikan*
depilatory cream	脱毛クリーム	*datsumoh-kreem*
deposit	手付け金／頭金	*te-tsuke-kin/atama-kin*
deposit (for safekeeping)	保管	*hokan*
dessert	デザート	*dezahto*
destination	行き先	*yuki-saki*
destination (terminal)	終点	*shooten*
develop (photo)	現像する	*genzoh suru*
diabetic	糖尿病患者	*toh-nyoh-byoh kanja*
dial	ダイヤル	*digh-yaru*
diamond	ダイヤモンド	*digh-a-mondo*
diarrhoea	下痢	*geri*
dictionary	辞典	*jiten*
diesel/diesel oil	ティーゼル	*deezeru*
diet	ダイエット	*digh-etto*
difficulty	困難	*kon-nan*
dining room	食堂	*shoku-doh*
dining/buffet car	食堂車／ビュッフェカー	*shokudoh-sha/buffay-kah*
dinner	ディナー	*dinah*
dinner (to have)	ディナーを食べる	*dinah-o taberu*
dinner jacket	ディナー用ジャケット	*dinah-yoh jaketto*
direction	方向	*hohkoh*
directly	直接に	*choku-setsu-ni*
dirty	きたない／汚れた	*kita-nigh/yogoreta*
disabled	障害者	*shoh-gigh-sha*
disco	ディスコ	*disko*
discount	割引	*wari-biki*
dish	一皿／一品	*shto-sara/ippin*
dish of the day	今日の料理	*kyoh-no ryohri*
disinfectant	消毒剤	*shohdoku-zigh*
distance	距離	*kyori*
distilled water	蒸留水	*joh-ryoo-swee*
disturb	じゃまする	*jama suru*
disturbance	妨害	*boh-gigh*
dive	潜る	*moguru*
diving	スキンダイビング	*skin-dighbingu*
diving board	飛び込み台	*tobikomi-digh*
diving gear	スキンダイビング・セット	*skin-dighbingu-setto*

divorced	離婚した	rikon shta
DIY store	日曜大工店	nichiyoh-dighku-ten
dizzy	めまい	me-migh
do	する	suru
doctor	医者	isha
dog	犬	inu
doll	人形	ningyoh
domestic	国内	koku-nigh
done (cooked)	よく料理した	yoku ryohri shta
door	戸/ドア	to/doa
double	ダブル	daburu
down	下	shta
draught	すき間風	skima-kazay
draughts	チェッカー	chekkah
dream (verb)	(…を) 夢に見る	(... o) yumay-ni miru
dress	ドレス	dores
dressing gown	部屋着	heya-gi
drink (medicine)	薬を飲む	kusuri-o nomu
drink (verb)	飲む	nomu
drinking chocolate	ホットチョコレート	hotto-choko-rehto
drinking water	飲料水	inryoh-swee
drive	運転する	unten suru
driver	運転手	untenshu
driving licence	運転免許	unten menkyo
dry	かわいた	kawa-ita
dry (verb)	干す	hosu
dry clean	ドライクリーニング	drigh-kreeningu
dry cleaner's	洗濯屋/	sentakuya/
	クリーニング店	kreeningu-ten
dummy	おしゃぶり	oshaburi
during	…中	... choo
during (in the middle of)	…の間に	... no igh-da-ni
during the day	昼間	hiruma

E

ear	耳	mimi
ear, nose and throat specialist	耳鼻・咽喉科	jibi-inkoh-ka
earache	耳痛	jitsoo
eardrops	耳薬	mimi-kusuri
early	早い	haya-i
earrings	イヤリング	iyaringu
earth	土地	to-chi
earthenware	陶器	toh-ki
east	東	higashi
easy (simple)	簡単な/容易な	kantan-na/yoh-i-na
easy (to use)	便利な	benri-na
eat	食べる	taberu
eczema	湿疹	shisshin
eel	ウナギ	unagi
egg	卵	tamago
elastic band	ゴム	gomu
electric	電気 (の)	denki (no)
electricity	電気	denki
embassy	大使館	tigh-shikan
emergency brake	緊急ブレーキ	kinkyoo brayki
emergency exit	非常口	hijoh-guchi

emergency phone	非常電話	*hijoh denwa*
emery board	つめやすり	*tsumay-yasuri*
emperor	天皇	*ten-noh*
empty	からの	*kara-no*
engaged (on the phone)	話し中	*hanashi-choo*
engaged (to be married)	婚約した	*kon-yak-shta*
England	イギリス	*Igirisu*
English (language)	英語	*ay-go*
enjoy	楽しむ	*tano-shimu*
envelope	封筒	*footoh*
escort	コンパニオン	*kompanion*
evening	夕方	*yoo-gata*
evening wear	ディナースーツ／	*dinah soots (men)/*
	イブニングドレス	*eebuningu dores*
		(women)
event	事件／できごと	*jiken/dekigoto*
everything	全部	*zembu*
everywhere	どこにも	*doko-nimo*
examine	探る	*saguru*
excavation	発掘	*hakkuts*
excellent	優れた	*sugureta*
exchange	交換する	*kohkan suru*
exchange office	為替両替所	*kawase-ryoh-gae-jo*
exchange rate	為替レート	*kawase-rayto*
excursion	遊覧	*yooran*
exhibition	展覧会	*tenran-kigh*
exit	出口	*deguchi*
expenses	費用／経費	*hiyoh/kayhi*
expensive	高い	*ta-kigh*
explain	説明する	*setsumay suru*
express	急行電車	*kyookoh densha*
external	外	*soto*
eye	目	*me*
eye drops	目薬	*me-gusuri*
eye shadow	アイシャドー	*igh-shadoh*
eye specialist	眼科医／目医者	*ganka-i/me-isha*
eyeliner	アイライナー	*igh-righnah*

F

face	顔	*kao*
factory	工場	*koh-joh*
fall (verb)	ころぶ	*korobu*
family	家族	*kazoku*
famous	有名な	*yoo-may-na*
far away	遠く	*tohku*
farm	農家	*nohka*
farmer	お百姓	*ohyakusho*
fashion	ファッション	*fashon*
fast	速い	*ha-yigh*
father (other's)	お父さま	*o-toh-sama*
father (own)	父	*chichi*
fault	誤り	*ayamari*
fax (verb)	ファックスを送る	*fakkusu-o okuru*
February	二月	*ni-gats*
feel	感じる	*kanjiru*
feel like	好む	*konomu*
fence	垣根	*kaki-ne*

ferry	渡し船／ フェリーボート	*watashi-bunay/* *feree-bohto*
fever	熱	*netsu*
fill	詰める	*tsumeru*
fill out	書き込む	*kaki-komu*
filling	詰め物	*tsumemono*
film (cinema)	映画	*ayga*
film (photo)	フィルム	*firumu*
filter	フィルター	*firutah*
filter cigarette	フィルター付き タバコ	*firutah-tski tabako*
find	見つける	*mitsu-keru*
fine (money)	罰金	*bakkin*
finger	指	*yubi*
fire	火	*hi*
fire (on)	火事	*kaji*
fire brigade	消防	*shoh-boh*
fire escape	非常階段	*hijoh kigh-dan*
fire extinguisher	消火器	*shoh-ka-ki*
first (in line)	最初に	*sigh-sho-ni*
first (number one)	第一／一番	*dai-ichi/ichiban*
first aid	応急手当て	*ohkyoo te-atay*
first class	一等	*ittoh*
fish	魚	*sakana*
fish (verb)	釣をする	*tsuri-o suru*
fishing rod	釣竿	*tsuri-zao*
fitness centre	フィットネスセンター	*fitnes-sentah*
fitness training	フィットネス	*fitnes*
fitting room	試着室	*shichaku-shits*
fix (puncture)	パンクしたタイヤを 直す	*panku shta tigh-ya-o* *na-osu*
flag	旗	*hata*
flash	フラッシュ	*furash*
flat (apartment)	アパート	*apahto*
flea market	蚤の市	*nomi-no-ichi*
flight	飛行	*hikoh*
flight number	便名	*bin-may*
flood	大水	*ohmizu*
floor	階	*kigh*
flounder	カレイ	*karay*
flour	粉	*kona*
flu	インフルエンザ	*infruenza*
fly (insect)	ハエ	*ha-e*
fly (verb)	飛ぶ	*tobu*
fly-over	高架橋	*kohka-kyoh*
fog	霧	*kiri*
foggy (to be)	霧がかかる	*kiri-nga kakaru*
folkloristic	民族伝統の	*minzoku dentoh-no*
follow	従う	*shita-ga-u*
food (items)	食品	*shokuhin*
food (stuffs)	食料	*shoku-ryoh*
food poisoning	食中毒	*shoku-choodoku*
foot	足	*ashi*
forbidden	禁止	*kinshi*
forehead	額	*sh-tigh*
foreign	外国の	*gigh-koku-no*
forget	忘れる	*wasureru*

fork	フォーク	fohku
form	用紙	yohshi
forward (a letter)	転送する	ten-soh suru
fountain	噴水	fun-swee
frame	額縁	gaku-buchi
free (no charge)	無料	muryoh
free (unoccupied)	空いている	igh-tay iru
free time	暇	hima
freeze	凍る	kohru
French bread	フランスパン	furansu-pan
fresh	新鮮な	shinsen-na
Friday	金曜日	kin-yoh-bi
fried	焼いた	yigh-ta
fried egg	目玉焼き	medama-yaki
friend	友達	tomo-dachi
friendly	心からの／親切な	kokoro-kara-no/
		shinsetu-na
frightened	恐れる	osoreru
fringe	前髪	ma-e-gami
fruit	フルーツ／果物	froots/kudamono
fruit juice	ジュース	joosu
frying pan	フライパン	furigh-pan
full (tank)	満タン	mantan
fun	楽しい	tano-shee

G

gallery	画廊	garoh
game	ゲーム	gaym
garage (car repair)	修理屋	shoori-ya
garbage bag	ごみ袋	gomi-bukuro
garden	庭	niwa
gauze	ガーゼ	gahzay
gear	ギア	gee-a
gel	ジェル	jeru
get married	結婚する	kekkon suru
get off	下車する／降りる	gesha suru/oriru
gift	贈り物／ギフト	okuri-mono/gift
gilt	金メッキ	kin-mekki
ginger	ショウガ	shoh-ga
girl	女の子	onna-no ko
girlfriend	ガールフレンド	gahru-frendo
giro cheque	小切手	kogittay
glass	ガラス	garas
glass (drinking)	グラス／コップ	guras/koppu
glasses	眼鏡	me-ganay
glasses (sun-)	サングラス	san-guras
glide	グライダーに乗る	gu-righdah-ni noru
glove	手袋	te-bukuro
glue	のり	nori
gnat (mosquito)	蚊	ka
go	行く	iku
go back	戻る	modoru
go out	外出する	gigh-shuts suru
gold	金	kin
golf course	ゴルフ場	gorufu-jo
good afternoon/day	こんにちは	kon-nichi-wa
good evening/night	こんばんは	komban-wa

Word list

15

good morning	おはようございます	ohayoh goza-imas
good night	おやすみなさい	oyasumi-na-sigh
goodbye	さようなら	sayoh-nara
gram	グラム	gram
grandchild	孫	mago
grandfather (other's)	おじいさん	o-jee-san
grandfather (own)	祖父	sofu
grandmother (other's)	お婆さん	obahsan
grandmother (own)	祖母	sobo
grape juice	グレープ・ジュース	grayp joosu
grapefruit	グレープフルーツ	graypu-furoots
grapes	ブドウ	budoh
grave	墓	haka
greasy	脂の多い	abura-no oh-ee
green	緑の	midori-no
greet	挨拶する	igh-sats suru
grey	灰色の／ねずみ色の	high-iro-no/nezumi-iro-no
grey (hair)	白髪	haku-hats
grill	網焼きをする／グリルする	amiyaki-o suru/guriru suru
grilled	ローストした	rohst shta
grocer	食料品店	shokuryoh-hin-ten
ground	土地	tochi
group	グループ	guroop
guest house	民宿／ペンション	minshuku/penshon
guide (book)	案内書	annigh-sho
guide (person)	ガイド	gigh-do
guided tour	ガイド付きツアー	gigh-do tsuki tsu-ah
gynaecologist	産婦人科	san-fujin-ka

H

hair	髪	kami
hairbrush	ヘアブラシ	hea-burashi
hairdresser	床屋／美容院	tokoya/biyoh-in
hairpins	ヘアピン	hea-pin
hairspray	ヘア・スプレー	hea-spray
half	半分	hambun
half full	…を半分	... o hambun
hammer	かなずち	kana-zuchi
hand	手	te
hand brake	ハンド・ブレーキ	hando-burayki
handbag	ハンドバッグ	hando-baggu
handkerchief	ハンカチ	hankachi
handmade	手作り	te-zukuri
happy	嬉しい	ure-shee
harbour	港	minato
hard	堅い	ka-tigh
hat	帽子	bohshi
hay fever	花粉症	kafun-shoh
head	頭	atama
headache	頭痛	zutsoo
health	健康	kenkoh
health food shop	自然食品店	shizen shoku-hin-ten
hear	聞く	kiku
hearing aid	補聴器	hochoh-ki
heart	心臓	shinzoh

heart patient	心臓病患者	*shinzoh-byoh kanja*
heat	熱さ	*atsusa*
heater	ヒーター	*heetah*
heavy	重い	*omo-i*
heel	かかと	*kakato*
hello	こんにちは	*kon-nichi-wa*
helmet	ヘルメット	*herumetto*
help	助け	*tasukay*
help	助ける／手伝う	*tas-keru/tetsu-dau*
helping (of food)	一人前	*shtori-migh*
herbal tea	ハーブティー	*hahbu-tee*
herbs (seasonings)	調味料	*chohmi-ryoh*
here	ここ	*koko*
herring	ニシン	*nishin*
high	高い	*ta-kigh*
high tide	満潮	*manchoh*
highchair	子供用椅子	*kodomo-yoh isu*
hiking	ハイキング	*high-kingu*
hip	腰	*koshi*
hire	賃貸する／借りる	*chin-tigh suru/kariru*
hitchhike	ヒッチハイクをする	*hitchi-high-ku-o suru*
hobby	趣味	*shumi*
hold-up	強盗	*gohtoh*
holiday	休暇／休み	*kyooka/yasumi*
holiday (festival)	祭日	*sigh-jits*
holiday (public)	休日	*kyoo-jits*
holiday house	別荘	*bessoh*
holiday park	休暇村	*kyoo-ka mura*
homesickness	ホームシック	*hohm-shikku*
honest	正直な	*shoh-jiki-na*
honey	蜂蜜	*hachi-mitsu*
horizontal	水平の	*swee-hay-no*
horrible	大変	*tigh-hen*
horse	馬	*uma*
hospital	病院	*byoh-in*
hospitality	もてなし／接待	*mote-nashi/set-tigh*
hot	熱い／暑い	*atsu-i*
hot (bitter, sharp)	辛い	*ka-righ*
hot spring	温泉	*onsen*
hotel	ホテル	*hoteru*
hot-water bottle	湯たんぽ	*yoo-tampo*
hour	時間	*jikan*
house	家／うち	*ie/uchi*
household items	家庭用品	*katay yoh-hin*
houses of parliament	国会議事堂	*kok-kigh giji-doh*
housewife	主婦	*shufu*
how far?	どのくらい （遠い）	*dono gurigh (toh-i)*
how long?	どのくらい （長い）	*dono gurigh (na-gigh)*
how much?	いくら	*ikura*
how?	どう	*doh*
hungry (to be)	空腹だ	*koofuku-da*
hurry	急速	*kyoosoku*
husband (other's)	ご主人	*goshujin*
husband (own)	夫／主人	*otto/shujin*
hut	小屋	*koya*

I

ice cubes	氷	kohri
ice skate	スケートをする	skehto-o suru
icecream	アイスクリーム	ighs-kreem
idea	考え	kan-ga-e
identification (card)	身分証明書	mibun shoh-may-sho
identify	身分を証明する	mibun-o shoh-may suru
ignition key	始動キー	shidoh kee
ill	病気	byoh-ki
illness	病気	byoh-ki
imagine	想像する	sohzoh suru
immediately	すぐに	sugu-ni
import duty	輸入税	yunyoo-zay
impossible	無理な／不可能な	muri-na/fukanoh-na
in	…の中に	....no naka-ni
in the evening	夕方	yoogata
in the morning	午前	gozen
included	…を含めて	.... o fukumete
included	含めた	fukumeta
indicate	示す	shi-mes
indicator	方向指示器	hohkoh-shijiki
industrial art	工芸	koh-gay
inexpensive	安い	yasu-i
infection	伝染	densen
(viral, bacterial)	(ビールスの、バクテリアの)	(beerus-no, bakuteria-no)
inflammation	炎症	enshoh
information	情報	joh-hoh
information (guide)	案内	an-nigh
information (material)	資料	shiryoh
information office	案内所	an-nigh-sho
injection	注射	choosha
injured	負傷した	f-shoh shta
inner tube	チューブ	choob
innocent	無罪な	mu-zigh-na
insect	こん虫	konchoo
insect bite	虫さされ	mushi-sasaray
insect repellant	虫除けクリーム	mushi-yokay kreem
inside	中に／内に	naka-ni/uchi-ni
insole	靴の内底	kutsu-no nigh-tay
instructions	使用法	shiyoh-hoh
insurance	保険	hoken
intermission	休憩	kyookay
international	国際の	koku-sigh-no
interpreter	通訳者	tsooyakusha
intersection	交差点	kohsaten
introduce (oneself)	紹介する	shoh-kigh suru
invite	招待する	shoh-tigh suru
iodine	赤チン	aka-chin
Ireland	アイルランド	igh-ru-rando
iron (clothes)	アイロン	igh-ron
iron (metal)	鉄	tetsu
iron (verb)	アイロンをかける	igh-ron-o kakeru
ironing board	アイロン台	igh-ron-digh
island	島	shima
itch	かゆい	kayui

J

jack	ジャッキ	*jakki*
jacket	ジャケット	*jaketto*
jam	ジャム	*jamu*
January	一月	*ichi-gats*
Japanese-style bar	居酒屋	*izakaya*
jaw	顎	*ago*
jellyfish	クラゲ	*kuragay*
jeweller	貴金属店／宝石店	*kikinzoku-ten/ hohseki-ten*
jewellery	装身具	*soh-shin-gu*
jog	ジョギング	*joggingu*
joke	冗談	*joh-dan*
juice	ジュース	*joosu*
July	七月	*shich-gats*
jumper	セーター	*sehtah*
June	六月	*roku-gats*

K

key	キー／鍵	*kee/kagi*
kilo	キロ（グラム）	*kiro(gram)*
kilometre	キロ（メートル）	*kito(mehtoru)*
kiss	キス	*kisu*
kiss (verb)	キスする	*kisu suru*
kitchen	台所	*digh-dokoro*
knee	膝	*hiza*
knee socks	ニー・ソックス／ ハイソックス	*nee-sokkusu/high-sokkusu*
knife	ナイフ	*nighfu*
knit	編む	*amu*
know	知る	*shiru*

L

lace	レース	*raysu*
lace (shoes)	靴ひも	*kutsu-himo*
ladies'	婦人用トイレ	*fujinyoh toy-ray*
lake	湖	*mizu-umi*
lamp	ランプ	*ramp*
land (ground)	土地	*tochi*
land (verb)	着陸する	*chaku-riku suru*
lane (of traffic)	車線	*shasen*
language	言葉／言語	*kotoba/gengo*
large	大きい	*ohkee*
last	最後／最終	*sigh-go/sigh-shoo*
last night	昨晩	*sakuban*
late	遅い	*oso-i*
later	後程	*nochi hodo*
laugh	笑う	*wara-u*
launderette	コインランドリー	*koyn randoree*
law	法律	*hohrits*
laxative	下剤	*ge-zigh*
leak (air)	パンク	*panku*
leather	皮	*kawa*
leather goods	皮製品	*kawa-say-hin*
leave	出発する	*shuppats suru*
leek	長ネギ	*naga-negi*
left	左	*hidari*

left (to turn)	左に曲がる	*hidari-ni magaru*
left luggage	手荷物一時預かり所	*te-nimots ichi-ji azukari-jo*
leg	足	*ashi*
lemon	レモン	*remon*
lend	…に貸す	*... ni kasu*
lens	レンズ	*renz*
less	少なく	*sku-naku*
lesson	レッスン	*ressun*
letter	手紙	*tegami*
lettuce	レタス	*retasu*
level crossing	踏切	*fumi-kiri*
library	図書館	*toshokan*
lie	うそ	*uso*
lie (down)	横になっている	*yoko-ni nattay iru*
lie (to tell a)	うそをつく	*uso-o tsku*
lift (hitchhike)	ヒッチハイク	*hitchi-high-ku*
lift (in building)	エレベーター	*ere-baytah*
lift (ski)	リフト	*rifto*
light	ライト	*righ-to*
light (not dark)	明るい	*aka-rui*
light (not heavy)	軽い	*ka-rui*
lighter	ライター	*righ-tah*
lighthouse	灯台	*toh-digh*
lightning	稲妻／稲光／かみなり	*inazuma/ina-bikari/ kaminari*
like (verb)	好む／好き	*konomu/ski*
line	線	*sen*
linen	麻／リネン	*asa/rinen*
lipstick	口紅	*kuchi-beni*
liqueur	リキュール	*rikyooru*
listen	聞く	*kiku*
literature	文学	*bun-gaku*
litre	リットル	*rittoru*
little (amount)	少ない	*sku-nigh*
live	住む	*sumu*
lobster	伊勢えび	*isay-ebi*
lock	鍵／錠前	*kagi/johma-e*
long	長い	*na-gigh*
look	見る	*miru*
look for	捜す	*sagasu*
look up	調べる	*shiraberu*
lorry	トラック	*torakku*
lose (verb)	失う／なくす	*ushina-u/nakusu*
loss	損失	*sonshits*
lost	失った	*ushinatta*
lost (to be)	道に迷う	*michi-ni mayo-u*
lost item	遺失物	*ish-ts-buts*
lost property office	遺失物取扱所	*ish-ts-buts tori-atsu-kigh-jo*
lotion	ローション	*rohshon*
loud (voice)	大声で	*ohgo-e-de*
love	愛／愛情	*igh/aigh-joh*
love (verb)	愛する	*igh-suru*
love with (to be in)	愛している	*igh-shtay iru*
low	低い	*hiku-i*
low tide	干潮／引き潮	*kanchoh/hiki-shio*

LPG	プロパン	propan
luck	幸運	koh-un
luggage	荷物	nimots
luggage locker	コイン・ロッカー	koyn rokkah
lumps (sugar)	角砂糖	kaku-zatoh
lunch	昼食	choo-shoku
lunch room (cafe)	コーヒーショップ／喫茶店	koh-hee-shoppu/ kissaten
lungs	肺	high

M

macaroni	マカロニ	makaroni
madam	…さん	...-san
magazine	雑誌	zasshi
mail	郵便	yoobin
main post office	郵便局本局／中央郵便局	yoobin-kyoku hon-kyoku /choo-oh yoobin-kyoku
main road	大通り	ohdohri
make an appointment	約束する	yak-soku suru
make love	セックスする	sekkusu suru
makeshift	一時的な	ichiji-teki-na
man	男	otoko
manager (caretaker)	管理人	kanri-nin
mandarin	ミカン	mikan
manicure	マニキュア	manikyua
many	たくさん	tak-san
map	地図	chizu
marble	大理石	digh-ri-seki
March	三月	san-gats
margarine	マーガリン	mahgarin
marina	ヨット用ドック／マリーナ	yotto-yoh dokku/mareena
market	市場／マーケット	ichiba/mahketto
marriage	結婚	kekkon
married	結婚した	kekkon shta
mass	ミサ	misa
massage	マッサージ	massahji
match	試合	shi-igh
matches	マッチ	matchi
matt (photo)	光沢のない	kohtaku-no nigh
May	五月	go-gats
maybe	多分	tabun
mayonnaise	マヨネーズ	mayonehzu
mayor	市長	shi-choh
meal	食事	shokuji
mean (verb)	意味する	imi suru
meat	肉	niku
medication	薬／薬品	kusuri/yakuhin
medicine	薬品／薬	yakuhin/kusuri
medicine for diarrhea	下痢止め	geri-dome
meet	…に会う	... ni au
melon	メロン	meron
melon (water)	西瓜	sweeka
membership (card)	会員証	kigh-in-shoh
menstruate	月経がある	gekkay-ga-aru
menstruation	生理／メンス	sayri/mensu

menu	メニュー／献立	menyoo/kondatay
menu of the day	本日のメニュー	honjitsu no menyoo
message	伝言	dengon
metal	金属	kinzoku
meter (in taxi)	メーター	mehtah
metre (100 cm)	メートル	mehtoru
migraine	偏頭痛	henzutsoo
mild (tobacco)	軽い	karui
milk	牛乳／ミルク	gyoo-nyoo/miruku
millimetre	ミリ	miri
	（メートル）	(mehtoru)
mince	挽き肉	hiki-niku
mineral water	ミネラルウォーター	mineraru-wohtah
minute	分	fun
mirror	鏡	kagami
miss (a person)	寂しくなる	sabishku-naru
missing (to be)	不足する	fusoku suru
missing person	迷子	migh-go
mistake	間違い	machi-gigh
mistaken (to be)	間違える	machi-ga-eru
misunderstanding	誤解	go-kigh
mixture (medicine)	飲み薬	nomi-gusuri
mocha	モカ	moka
modern art	現代の芸術	gen-digh-no gay-juts
molar	奥歯	okuba
moment	瞬間	shunkan
moment (just a)	ちょっと	chotto
monastery	修道院	shoodoh-in
Monday	月曜日	gets-yohbi
money	お金	o-kanay
month	月	tski
moped	モペット	mopetto
motel	モーテル	mohteru
mother (other's)	お母さま	o-kah-sama
mother (own)	母	haha
motor cross	モトクロス	moto-kurosu
motorbike	バイク	bighk
motorboat	モーターボート	mohtah-bohto
motorway	高速道路	kohsoku dohro
mountain	山	yama
mountain hut	山小屋	yama-goya
mountaineering	登山	toh-zan
mountaineering shoes	登山靴	toh-zan-guts
mouse	ネズミ	nezumi
mouth	口	kuchi
much	たくさん	tak-san
multi-storey car park	駐車場	choosha-jo
muscle	筋	suji
muscle spasms	筋肉けいれん	kinniku kayren
museum	美術館／博物館	bijutsu-kan/
		hakubutsu-kan
mushrooms	キノコ	kinoko
music	音楽	on-gaku
musical	ミュージカル	myoojikaru
mussels	イガイ／ムール貝	i-gigh/mooru-gigh
mustard	からし／	karashi/mastahdo
	マスタード	

N

nail	釘	kugi
nail (finger)	つめ	tsumay
nail scissors	つめ切り	tsumay-kiri
naked	裸／ヌード	hadaka/noodo
nappy	おしめ	o-shimay
nationality	国籍	koku-seki
natural	自然の	shizen-no
nature	自然	shizen
naturism	裸体主義	ra-tigh-shugi
nauseous	気分が悪い	kibun-nga waru-i
near	…の近くに	... no chikaku-ni
nearby	ごく近く	goku-chikaku
necessary	…が必要	... nga hitsuyoh
neck	首	kubi
necklace	ネックレス	nekkuraysu
needle	針	hari
negative (photo)	ネガ	nega
neighbours	隣の人	tonari-no shto
nephew	甥	oi
never	全然…ない／	zenzen ... nigh/
	全く…ない	mattaku ... nigh
new	新しい	atara-shee
news	ニュース	nyoos
news stand	キオスク／売店	kiosk/bigh-ten
newspaper	新聞	shimbun
next	次の	tsugi-no
next to	…のそばに	... no soba-ni
nice	楽しい／快適な	tanoshee/kigh-teki-na
nice (friendly)	親切	shin-sets
nice (happy)	うれしい	ureshee
nice (person)	かわいい／よい	kawa-ee/yoi
nice (taste)	おいしい	oi-shee
niece	姪	may
night	夜	yoru
night duty	夜勤	yakin
nightclub	ナイト・クラブ	nighto-kurabu
nipple (bottle)	乳首	chi-kubi
no	いいえ	ii-ye
no overtaking	追い越し禁止	oi-koshi kinshi
noise	うるさい／騒音	uru-sigh/soh-on
nonstop (plane)	直行	chokkoh
no-one	だれも…ない	daray-mo ... nigh
normal	普通	futsoo
north	北	kita
nose	鼻	hana
nose drops	鼻薬	hana-gusuri
note pad	メモ帳	memo-cho
notepaper	便箋	binsen
nothing	何も…ない	nani-mo ... nigh
November	十一月	joo-ichi-gats
nowhere	どこにも…ない	doko-nimo ... nigh
nude beach	ヌーディスト・ビーチ	noodisto beech
number	番号	ban-go
number plate	ナンバー・プレート	nanbah-purayto
nurse	看護婦	kangofu

nutmeg	ナツメッグ	natsumeggu
nuts	ナッツ／おつまみ	nattsu/otsumami

O

October	十月	joo-gats
off (gone bad)	くさった	kusatta
offer	申し出る	mohshi-deru
office	事務所／オフィス	jimusho/ofiss
off-licence	酒屋	saka-ya
oil	油／オイル	abura/oiru
oil level	オイルの量	oiru-no ryoh
ointment	軟膏	nankoh
ointment for burns	火傷の軟膏	yakedo-no nanko
okay	OK	OK
old (thing/person)	古い／年とった	furui/toshi-totta
olive oil	オリーブ油	oreebu-yoo
olives	オリーブ	oreebu
omelette	オムレツ	omurets
on	…の上に	... no ue-ni
on board (to go)	乗船する	johsen suru
on the right	右の方に	migi-no hoh-ni
on the way	途中で	tochoo-de
oncoming car	対向車	tigh-koh-sha
one-way traffic	一方通行	ippoh tsookoh
onion	玉ねぎ	tama-negi
open (to be)	開いている	ightay-iru
open (verb)	開ける	akeru
opera	オペラ	opera
operate (surgeon)	手術する	shujuts suru
operator (telephone)	交換手	kohkanshu
opposite	向こう側	mukoh-gawa
optician	眼鏡屋	megane-ya
orange	オレンジ	orenji
orange (colour)	オレンジ色	orenji-iro
orange juice	オレンジ・ジュース	orenji-joosu
order	注文	choomon
order (tidy)	片づいた	kata-zuita
order (verb)	注文する	choomon suru
other	他の	hoka-no
other side	向こう側	mukoh-gawa
outside	外	soto
over there	あそこ	asoko
overtake	追い越す	oi-kosu
oysters	カキ	kaki

P

packed lunch	弁当	bentoh
page	ページ	payji
pain	痛み	itami
painkiller	痛み止め／鎮痛剤	itami-domay/ chin-tsoo-zigh
paint	ペンキ	penki
painting	絵画	kigh-ga
palace	宮殿／皇居	kyooden/kohkyo
pan	鍋	nabay
pancake	パンケーキ	pan-kehki
pancake (Japanese style)	ホットケーキ	hotto-kehki

pane	窓ガラス	*mado-garas*
pants	ズボン／スラックス	*zubon/surakks*
paper	紙	*kami*
paprika	ピーマン	*peeman*
paraffin oil	パラフィン油／灯油	*parafin-yoo/tohyoo*
parasol	日傘	*higasa*
parcel	小包み	*ko-zutsu-mi*
pardon	すみません	*sumimasen*
parents (other's)	ご両親	*go-ryohshin*
parents (own)	両親	*ryohshin*
park	公園	*koh-en*
park (verb)	駐車する	*choosha suru*
parking space (metre)	駐車メーター	*choosha mehtah*
parsley	パセリ	*paseri*
part (car-)	部品	*buhin*
partner	恋人	*koi-bito*
party	パーティー	*pahtay*
passable (road)	通行出来る	*tsoo-koh dekiru*
passenger	旅客	*ryokyaku*
passport	パスポート	*pasupohto*
passport photo	証明写真	*shoh-may shashin*
patient	病人	*byohnin*
pavement	歩道	*hodoh*
pay	払う	*hara-u*
pay the bill	勘定を払う	*kanjoh-o hara-u*
peach	桃	*momo*
peanuts	ピーナッツ	*peenattsu*
pear	梨	*nashi*
peas	グリーンピース	*gureenpeesu*
pedal	ペダル	*pedaru*
pedestrian crossing	横断歩道	*ohdan-hodoh*
pedicure	ペディキュア	*pedikyua*
pedometer	万歩計	*mampo-kay*
pen	ペン	*pen*
pencil	鉛筆	*empits*
penis	ペニス	*penis*
pepper	胡椒	*koshoh*
performance	上演	*joh-en*
perfume	香水	*kohswe*
perm	パーマ（ネント）	*pahma (nento)*
perm (verb)	パーマをかける	*pahma-o kakeru*
permit	許可書	*kyoka-sho*
person	…人	*...-nin*
personal	個人的	*kojinteki*
petrol	ガソリン	*gasorin*
petrol station	ガソリンスタンド	*gasorin stando*
pets	ペット	*petto*
pharmacy	薬局	*yak-kyok*
phone (tele-)	電話	*denwa*
phone (verb)	電話をかける	*denwa-o kakeru*
phone box	電話ボックス	*denwa bokkusu*
phone directory	電話帳	*denwa-choh*
phone number	電話番号	*denwa-ban-goh*
photo	写真	*shashin*
photocopier	コピーマシン	*kopee-mashin*
photocopy	コピー	*kopee*
photocopy (verb)	コピーする	*kopee suru*

pick up (come to)	取りに来る	*tori-ni kuru*
pick up (go to)	取って来る	*tottay kuru*
picnic	ピクニック	*pikunikku*
pier	埠頭	*f-toh*
pigeon	ハト	*hato*
pill (contraceptive)	避妊薬／ピル	*hi-nin-yaku/piru*
pillow	枕	*makura*
pillowcase	枕カバー	*makura-kabah*
pin	ピン／留め針	*pin/tomebari*
pineapple	パイナップル	*pighn-appuru*
pipe	パイプ	*pighpu*
pipe tobacco	パイプ用たばこ	*pighpu-yoh tabako*
pity	残念	*zannen*
place of interest	みどころ／観光地	*midokoro/kankoh-chi*
plan	計画	*kay-kaku*
plant	植物	*shokubuts*
plasters	バンソウコウ	*bansohkoh*
plastic	プラスチック	*puraschik*
plastic bag	ビニール袋	*bineeru-bukuro*
plate	皿	*sara*
platform	（プラット）ホーム	*(puratto) hohmu*
play	劇	*geki*
play (verb)	遊ぶ	*asobu*
play golf	ゴルフをする	*gorufu-o suru*
play sport	スポーツをする	*spohts-o suru*
play tennis	テニスをする	*tenisu-o suru*
playground	遊園地	*yoo-en-chi*
playing cards	トランプ	*torampu*
pleasant	気持ちのよい	*kimochi-no-yoi*
please	お願いします	*o-ne-gigh-shimas*
pleasure	楽しみ	*tano-shimi*
plum	梅	*umay*
pocketknife	ポケットナイフ	*poketto-nighfu*
point	指さす	*yubi sasu*
poison	毒	*doku*
police	警察	*kay-sats*
police station	警察署／交番	*kay-satsu-sho/kohban*
policeman	警察官／おまわりさん	*kaysats-kan/omawari-san*
pond	池	*ikay*
pony	ポニー馬	*ponee-uma*
population	人口	*jinkoh*
pork	豚肉	*buta-niku*
port	ポートワイン	*pohto-wighn*
porter	赤帽	*akaboh*
porter (concierge)	門番／守衛	*momban/shu-ay*
post code	郵便番号	*yoobin ban-go*
post office	郵便局	*yoobin-kyoku*
postage	郵便料金	*yoobin ryohkin*
postbox	ポスト／郵便箱	*posto /yoobin bako*
postcard	葉書／絵葉書	*hagaki/e-hagaki*
postman	郵便屋さん	*yoobin-ya-san*
potato	ジャガイモ	*jaga-imo*
poultry	家禽	*kakin*
powdered milk	粉ミルク	*kona-miruku*
power point	コンセント	*konsento*
pram	乳母車／ベビーカー	*ubaguruma/baybee-kah*

prawns	小エビ	*ko-ebi*
precious	貴重	*kichoh*
prefer	…方が好きだ	*... hoh-nga ski da*
preference	好み	*konomi*
pregnant	妊娠	*nin-shin*
prescription	処方	*shohoh*
present (not absent)	出席	*shus-seki*
present (gift)	プレゼント	*purezento*
press	押す	*osu*
pressure	圧力	*atsu-ryoku*
price	値段	*nedan*
price list	値段表	*nedan-hyoh*
print	プリント	*printo*
print (verb)	プリントする	*printo suru*
probably	多分	*tabun*
problem	問題	*mon-digh*
profession	職業	*shoku-gyoh*
programme	プログラム	*program*
pronounce	発音する	*hatsuon suru*
propane camping gas	プロパン・ガス	*propan-gas*
pudding (caramel)	プディング／プリン	*pudingu/purin*
pull	引く	*hiku*
pull a muscle	筋肉を痛める	*kin-niku-o itameru*
pulse	脈	*myaku*
pure	純粋な	*junswee-na*
purple	紫色	*murasaki-iro*
purse	ハンドバッグ	*hando-baggu*
purse (money)	サイフ	*sigh-f*
push	押す	*osu*
puzzle	なぞ／パズル	*nazo/pazuru*
pyjamas	パジャマ	*pajama*

Q

quarter	四分の一	*yombun-no ichi*
quarter of an hour	十五分	*joo-gofun*
queen	女王	*jo-oh*
question	質問	*shitsumon*
quick	速く	*hayaku*
quiet	静かな	*shizuka-na*

R

radio	ラジオ	*rajio*
railways	鉄道	*tetsudoh*
rain	雨	*amay*
rain (verb)	雨が降る	*amay-ga furu*
raincoat	レインコート	*rayn-kohto*
raisins	干ぶどう	*hoshi-budoh*
rape	強姦	*gohkan*
rapids	急流	*kyooryoo*
raspberries	木イチゴ	*ki-ichigo*
raw	生の	*nama-no*
raw ham	生ハム	*nama-hamu*
raw vegetables	生の野菜	*nama-no ya-sigh*
razor blades	かみそり	*kamisori*
read	読む	*yomu*
ready	用意の出来た	*yoh-i-no dekita*
really	ほんとうに	*hontoh-ni*

receipt	領収書／受取書	ryoh-shuh-sho/ uketorisho
recipe	料理法	ryohri-hoh
reclining chair	リクライニング・チェア	rikrighning chea
recommend	推薦する	sweesen suru
rectangle	長方形	choh-hoh-kay
red	赤い	a-kigh
red wine	赤ワイン	aka-wighn
reduction	減少	genshoh
refrigerator	冷蔵庫	rayzoh-ko
regards	…によろしく	... ni yoroshku
region	地方	chihoh
registered	書留	kaki-tomay
relatives	家族	kazoku
reliable	確かな	tash-ka-na
religion	宗教	shoo-kyoh
rent out	賃貸する	chin-tigh suru
repair	修理をする	shoori-o suru
repairs	修理	shoori
repeat	繰り返す	kuri-ka-esu
report (police)	調書	choh-sho
responsible	責任がある	sekinin-ga aru
rest	休憩する／休む	kyookay suru/yasumu
restaurant	レストラン	resutoran
result	結果	kekka
retired	退職した	tigh-shoku shta
return (ticket)	往復（切符）	ohf-ku (kippu)
reverse (vehicle)	バックする	bakk suru
rheumatism	リューマチ	ryoomachi
rice (cooked)	ごはん	gohan
rice (grain)	米	komay
ridiculous	ばかな／よしたまえ	baka-na/yoshi-tama-e
riding (horseback)	乗馬	johba
riding school	乗馬学校	johba gakkoh
right	右	migi
right of way	優先	yoosen
ripe	熟した	juku shta
risk	危険	kiken
river	川	kawa
road	道路	dohro
roadway	自動車道	jidohsha-doh
roasted	焼いた	yigh-ta
rock	岩	iwa
roll	ロールパン	rohru-pan
roof rack	ルーフ・ラック	roof-rakku
room	部屋	he-ya
room number	部屋番号	he-ya ban-go
room service	ルーム・サービス	room sahbis
rope	紐／ロープ	himo/rohp
rosé (wine)	ロゼ	rozay
roundabout	ロータリー	rohtaree
route	道	michi
rowing boat	ボート	bohto
rubber	ゴム	gomu
rude	失礼な	shits-ray-na
ruins	廃虚	high-kyo

| run into | …に出会う | ... ni de-au |
| running shoes | スポーツ・シューズ | spohts-shooz |

s

sad	悲しい	kana-shee
safe	安全な	anzen-na
safe	金庫	kinko
safety pin	安全ピン	anzen-pin
sail (verb)	ヨットを走らせる	yotto-o hashiraseru
sailing boat	ヨット	yotto
salad	サラダ	sarada
salad oil	サラダ油	sarada-yoo
salami	サラミソーセージ	sarami sohsehji
sale	売り出し	uridashi
salt	塩	shio
same	同じ	onaji
sandy beach	砂浜	suna-hama
sanitary pad	生理用ナプキン	sayri-yoh napkin
sardines	イワシ	iwashi
satisfied	満足した	manzoku shta
Saturday	土曜日	do-yoh-bi
sauce	ソース	sohsu
sauna	サウナ	sauna
sausage	ソーセージ	sohsehji
say	言う	yoo
scarf	スカーフ／マフラー	skahf/mafurah
scenic walk	散歩道	sampo-michi
school	学校	gakkoh
scissors	はさみ	hasami
scooter	スクーター	skootah
Scotland	スコットランド	Skottorando
scrambled eggs	煎り卵	iri-tamago
screw	ねじ	neji
screwdriver	ねじ回し／ドライバー	neji-mawashi/dorighbah
sculpture	彫刻	choh-kok
sea	海	umi
seasick	船酔い	funa-yoi
seat	座席	zaseki
second	秒	byoh
second (in line)	第二	digh-ni
second-hand	中古品	chooko-hin
sedative	鎮静剤	chinsay-zigh
see	見る	miru
see (go sightseeing)	観光に行く	kankoh-ni iku
self-timer	セルフ・タイマー	serufu-tighmah
send	送る	okuru
sentence	文章	bunshoh
September	九月	ku-gats
serious	深刻な	shinkoku-na
service	サービス	sahbis
serviette	ナプキン	napukin
set	セット	setto
sewing needs	裁縫道具	sigh-hoh dohgu
shade	陰	kagay
shallow	浅い	a-sigh
shammy	セーム皮	sehmu-gawa
shampoo	シャンプー	shampoo

shark	サメ／フカ	samay/f-ka
shave	剃る	soru
shaver	シェーバー／	shaybah/denki
	電気かみそり	kamisori
shaving brush	ひげ剃り用ブラシ	hige-sori-yoh burashi
shaving cream	シェービング・	shaybingu-kureemu
	クリーム	
shaving soap	ひげ剃り用石けん	hige-sori-yoh sekken
sheet	シーツ	sheets
sherry	シェリー	she-ree
shirt	シャツ	shats
shoe	靴	ku-tsu
shoe polish	靴クリーム	kutsu-kureemu
shoe shop	靴屋	ku-tsu-ya
shoemaker	靴直し	kutsu-naoshi
shop	店	misay
shop (verb)	買い物をする	kigh-mono-o suru
shop assistant	販売員／店員	han-bigh-in/ten-in
shop window	ショーウィンドー	shoh-windoh
shopping centre	ショッピングセンター	shoppingu-sentah
short	短い	miji-kigh
short circuit	ショート	shohto
shorts	半ズボン	han-zubon
shoulder	肩	kata
show	ショー／上演	shoh/joh-en
shower	シャワー	shawah
shutter	シャッター	shattah
sieve	ふるい	furui
sign (name)	署名する	shomay suru
sign (road)	交通標識	kohtsoo hyoh-shiki
signature	署名／サイン	sho-may/sign
silence	沈黙／静けさ	chinmoku/shizukesa
silver	銀	gin
silver-plated	銀メッキの	ginmekki-no
simple	単純な	tanjun-na
single	シングル	shinguru
single (one way)	片道	katamichi
single (unmarried)	独身の	dokushin-no
sir	…さん	...-san
sister (elder, other's)	お姉さん	o-nay-san
sister (elder, own))	姉	anay
sister (younger, other's)	妹さん	imohto-san
sister (younger, own)	妹	imohto
sit	座る	suwaru
size	サイズ	sighzu
ski	スキーする	skee suru
ski boots	スキー靴	skee-gutsu
ski goggles	スキー用ゴーグル	skee-yoh gohguru
ski instructor	スキー指導員	skee shidoh-in
ski lessons/class	スキーレッスン／	skee ressun/
	教室	kyoh-shtsu
ski lift	スキーリフト	skee-rifuto
ski pants	スキーズボン／	skee-zubon/
	スキー用パンツ	skee-yoh pants
ski slope	ゲレンデ	gerenday
ski stick	ストック	stokku
ski suit	スキースーツ	skee-soots

ski wax	スキー用ワックス	skee-yoh wakkusu
skin	肌	hada
skirt	スカート	sukahto
skis	スキー	skee
sleep	眠る	nemuru
sleeping car	寝台車	shin-digh-sha
sleeping pills	睡眠薬	sui-min-yaku
slide	スライド	su-righdo
slip	シミーズ／	shimeez/petikohto
	ペティコート	
slow	ゆっくり	yukkuri
slow train	各駅列車	kaku-eki ressha
small	小さい	chee-sigh
small change	小銭	kozeni
smell	臭う	ni-ou
smoke	煙	kemuri
smoked	薫製した	kunsay shta
smoking	喫煙	kitsu-en
smoking compartment	喫煙車	kitsu-en-sha
snake	ヘビ	hebi
snorkel	スノーケル	snohkeru
snow	雪	yuki
snow (verb)	雪が降る	yuki-ga furu
snow chains	チェーン	chayn
soap	石けん	sekken
soap box	石けん箱	sekken-bako
soap powder	粉石けん	kona-sekken
soccer	サッカー	sakkah
soccer match	サッカー試合	sakkah-ji-igh
socket	コンセント	konsento
socks	靴下／ソックス	kutsu-shta/sokkusu
soft drink	ソフト・ドリンク	sofut-dorinku
sole (fish)	舌びらめ	shta-biramay
sole (shoe)	靴底	kutsu-soko
solicitor	弁護士	ben-goshi
someone	誰か	daray-ka
sometimes	時々	toki-doki
somewhere	どこか	doko-ka
son (other's)	息子さん	mus-ko-san
son (own)	息子	mus-ko
soon	早く	hayaku
sorbet	シャーベット	shahbetto
sore	傷	kizu
sore throat	のどの痛み	nodo-no itami
sorry	すみません	sumimasen
soup	スープ	soop
sour	すっぱい	sup-pigh
sour cream	サワークリーム	sawah-kureemu
south	南	minami
souvenir	おみやげ／おみやげ品	omiyagay/omiyage-hin
soy sauce	醤油	shoh-yu
spaghetti	スパゲッティ	spagetti
spanner	スパナー	spanah
spare	予備	yobi
spare parts	予備部品	yobi-buhin
spare tyre	予備のタイヤ	yobi-no tigh-ya
spare wheel	予備の車輪	yobi-no sharin

speak	話す	*hanasu*
special	特別な	*tokubets-na*
specialist (doctor)	専門医	*semmon-i*
speciality (cooking)	特別料理	*tokubets ryohri*
speed limit	最高速度	*sigh-koh sokudo*
spell	つづる	*tsuzuru*
spicy	スパイシー	*spighshee*
splinter	とげ	*togay*
spoon	スプーン	*spoon*
sport	スポーツ	*spohtsu*
sports centre	スポーツ・センター	*spohts-sentah*
spot (place)	場所	*basho*
sprain	くじく	*kujiku*
spring	春	*haru*
square (plaza)	広場	*hiroba*
square (shape)	正方形	*sayhoh-kay*
square metres	平方メートル	*hayhoh mehtoru*
squash	スカッシュをする	*skahsh-o suru*
stadium	スタジアム	*stajiam*
stain	しみ	*shimi*
stain remover	しみ取り	*shimi-tori*
stairs	階段	*kigh-dan*
stamp	切手	*kittay*
start	動き出させる	*ugoki-dasaseru*
station	駅	*eki*
statue	像	*zoh*
stay (in hotel)	宿泊する	*shuku-haku suru*
stay (remain)	滞在	*tigh-zigh*
steal	盗む	*nusumu*
steel	鋼鉄	*kohtets*
stench	臭いにおい	*ku-sigh ni-oi*
sting (noun)	虫さされ	*mushi-sasaray*
stitch (med.)	（傷を）縫い合わせる	*(kizu-o) nui-awaseru*
stitch (verb)	縫う	*noo*
stock (soup)	スープの素	*soop-no moto*
stockings	ストッキング	*stokkingu*
stomach	胃	*i*
stomach (abdominal region)	腹／腹部	*hara/fukubu*
stomach ache	腹痛	*fuku-tsoo*
stomach cramps	激しい腹痛	*hageshee fuku-tsoo*
stools	糞便	*fumben*
stop	止まる	*tomaru*
stop (bus)	停留所／停車場	*tay-ryoo-jo/tay-sha-jo*
stopover	途中下車	*tochoo-gesha*
storm	嵐	*arashi*
straight	真っ直ぐ	*massugu*
straight ahead	真っ直ぐに	*massugu-ni*
straw	ストロー	*sutoroh*
strawberries	イチゴ	*ichigo*
street	道	*michi*
street side	道端	*michibata*
strike	スト（ライキ）	*suto (righki)*
strong	強い	*tsuyo-i*
study	勉強する	*benkyoh suru*
stuffing	詰め物	*ts-me-mono*
subtitled	字幕付きで	*jimaki-tski-de*

Word list

succeed	出来る	dekiru
sugar	砂糖	satoh
suit	スーツ	soots
suitcase	スーツケース	soots-kays
summer	夏	nats
sun	太陽	tigh-yoh
sun hat	日よけ帽	hiyoke-boh
sunbathe	日光浴	nikkoh-yoku
Sunday	日曜日	nichi-yoh-bi
sunglasses	サングラス	san-guras
sunrise	日の出	hinoday
sunset	日暮れ	higuray
sunstroke	日射病	nissha-byoh
suntan lotion	日焼け止めクリーム	hiyakedome kureemu
suntan oil	日焼けオイル	hiyake-oiru
supermarket	スーパー（マーケット）	soopah (mahketto)
surcharge	追加料金	tsuika ryohkin
surf	サーフィンをする	sahfin-o suru
surf board	サーフボード	sahfu-bohdo
surname	苗字	myoh-ji
surprise	驚き	odoroki
swallow	飲みこむ	nomi-komu
swamp	沼地	numa-chi
sweat	汗	asay
sweet	甘い	ama-i
sweet (kind)	親切な	shin-sets-na
sweet corn	トウモロコシ	toh-moro-koshi
sweets	お菓子／おやつ	okashi/oyats
swim	泳ぐ	oyogu
swimming pool	プール	pooru
swimming trunks	水泳パンツ	swee-ay pants
swindle	詐欺	sagi
switch	スイッチ	switchi
synagogue	ユダヤ教の会堂	yudayakyoh-no kigh-doh

T

table	テーブル	tehburu
table tennis	卓球／ピンポン	takkyoo/pin-pon
tablet	錠剤	joh-zigh
take (medicine)	服用する	fukuyoh suru
take (photograph)	（写真を）撮る	(shashin-o) toru
take (time)	時間がかかる	jikan-nga kakaru
talcum powder	タルカム・パウダー	tarukamu paudah
talk	話す	hanasu
tall	背が高い	say-nga ta-kigh
tampons	タンポン	tampon
tanned	日に焼けた	hi-ni yaketa
tap	蛇口	jaguchi
tap water	水道の水	sweedoh-no mizu
taste (verb)	試す	tamesu
taste	味	aji
tax free shop	免税店	menzay-ten
taxi	タクシー	takshee
taxi stand	タクシー乗り場	takshee noriba

tea	お茶	ocha
tea (black)	紅茶	kohcha
tea (green)	緑茶	ryokucha
tea ceremony	お茶会	ocha-kigh
teapot	急須／ティーポット	kyoosu/tee-pott
teaspoon	茶さじ／ティースプーン	chasaji/tee-spoon
telegram	電報	dempoh
telephoto lens	望遠レンズ	boh-en renzu
television	テレビ	terebi
telex	テレックス	terekkusu
temperature (body)	体温	tigh-on
temperature (heat)	温度	ondo
temperature (weather)	気温	kion
temporary filling	一時的な虫歯の詰め物	ichiji-teki-na mushiba-no tsumemono
tender	柔らかい	yawara-kigh
tennis ball	テニスボール	tenisu-bohru
tennis court	テニスコート	tenisu-kohto
tennis racket	テニスラケット	tenisu-raketto
tenpin bowling (to do)	ボーリングをする	bohring-o suru
tent	テント	tento
tent peg	ペグ	pegu
terrace	テラス	terasu
terribly	大変な	tigh-hen-na
thank	お礼を言う	oray-o yoo
thank you	ありがとうございます	arigatoh go-zigh-mas
thanks	ありがとう	arigatoh
thaw	溶ける	tokeru
the day after tomorrow	あさって	asattay
theatre	劇場	gekijo
theft	窃盗	settoh
there	そこ	soko
thermal bath	温泉	onsen
thermometer (body)	体温計	tigh-onkay
thermometer (weather)	温度計	ondokay
thick	太い	f-toy
thief	泥棒	doroboh
thigh	太腿	fto-momo
thin (not fat)	細い／痩せた	hoso-i/yaseta
thin (not thick)	薄い	usu-i
think	思う	omo-u
think (consider)	考える	kanga-eru
third ($\frac{1}{3}$)	三分の一	sambun no ichi
thirsty (to be)	のどが渇く	nodo-ga kawaku
this afternoon	今日の午後	kyoh-no gogo
this evening	今晩	komban
this morning	今日の午前	kyoh-no gozen
thread	糸	ito
throat	喉	nodo
throat lozenges	せき止めドロップ	seki-domay doroppu
throw up	吐く	haku
thunderstorm	雷雨	righ-u
Thursday	木曜日	moku-yohbi
ticket	切符	kippu
ticket (admission)	入場券	nyoo-joh-ken
ticket (travel)	切符	kippu

tickets (seat)	座席券	*zaseki-ken*
tidy	片付ける	*kata-zukeru*
tie	ネクタイ	*neku-tigh*
tights	パンスト	*pan-sto*
time	時間	*jikan*
times	回	*kigh*
timetable	時刻表	*jikoku-hyoh*
tin (tinned)	缶詰め	*kanzu-may*
tip	チップ	*chippu*
tissues	ティッシューペーパー	*tisshoo-pehpah*
toast	トースト	*tohsto*
tobacco	たばこ	*tabako*
toboggan	そり	*sori*
today	今日	*kyoh*
toe	足の指	*ashi-no yubi*
together	一緒に	*issho-ni*
toilet	トイレ／お手洗い／	*toiray/o-te-a-righ/*
	便所	*benjo*
toilet paper	トイレットペーパー	*toiretto-pehpah*
toilet seat	便座	*benza*
toiletries	化粧品	*keshoh-hin*
tomato	トマト	*tomato*
tomato puree	トマトピューレー	*tomato-pyooray*
tomato sauce	トマトケチャップ	*tomato-kechappu*
tomorrow	明日	*ashta*
tongue	舌	*shta*
tonic water	トニック	*tonikku*
tonight	今晩／今夜	*komban/konya*
tools	道具	*doh-gu*
tooth	歯	*ha*
toothache	歯痛	*ha-ita*
toothbrush	歯ブラシ	*ha-burashi*
toothpaste	歯磨	*ha-migaki*
toothpick	ようじ	*yohji*
top up	おかわり	*okawari*
total	全部	*zen-bu*
tough	固い	*ka-tigh*
tour	ツアー／周遊／旅行	*tsu-ah/shoo-yoo/*
		ryokoh
tour guide	案内者／ガイド	*an-nigh-sha/gighdo*
tourist class	二等	*nitoh*
Tourist Information office	観光案内所	*kankoh an-nigh-sho*
tow	牽引する	*ken-in suru*
tow cable	牽引ロープ	*ken-in rohpu*
towel	タオル／手拭い	*ta-oru/te-nugui*
tower	塔	*toh*
town	町	*machi*
town hall	市役所	*shiyakusho*
toys	おもちゃ	*omocha*
traffic	交通	*kohtsoo*
traffic light	信号	*shingo*
train	列車	*ressha*
train (electric)	電車	*densha*
train ticket	切符	*kippu*
train timetable	時刻表	*jikoku-hyoh*
translate	翻訳する	*hon-yaku suru*
travel	旅行する	*ryokoh suru*

travel agent	旅行代理店	ryokoh-dighri-ten
travel guide	旅行案内/案内書	ryokoh an-nigh/ an-nigh-sho
traveller	旅行者	ryokohsha
traveller's cheque	旅行用小切手	ryokoh-yoh kogittay
treacle/syrup	シロップ	shiroppu
treatment	治療	chi-ryoh
triangle	三角	sankaku
trim	切りそろえる	kiri-soro-eru
trip	旅行	ryokoh
trip (sightseeing)	観光	kankoh
trip (walk)	散歩	sampo
trout	マス(鱒)	masu
trunk call	長距離電話	choh-kyori denwa
trunk code	市外局番	shi-gigh kyokuban
trustworthy	たよりになる	tayori-ni naru
try on	試着する	shichaku suru
tube	チューブ	choob
Tuesday	火曜日	ka-yohbi
tumble drier	乾燥機	kansohki
tuna	マグロ	maguro
tunnel	トンネル	tonneru
turn	回	kigh
TV	テレビ	terebi
TV guide	テレビガイド	terebi gigh-do
tweezers	ピンセット	pinsetto
typhoon	台風	tigh-foo
tyre	タイヤ	tigh-ya
tyre pressure	タイヤ圧力	tigh-ya atsu-ryoku

U

ugly	みにくい/美しくない	minikui/utsu-kushiku-nigh
umbrella	傘	kasa
under	…の下に	... no shta-ni
underground	地下	chika
underground railway system	地下鉄	chikatets
underground station	地下鉄の駅	chikatets-no eki
underpants	パンツ	pants
understand	分かる/理解する	wakaru/ri-kigh suru
underwear	下着	shta-gi
undress	服を脱ぐ	fuku-o nugu
unemployed	失業	shits-gyoh
uneven (ground)	でこぼこの	dekoboko-no
university	大学	digh-gaku
unleaded	無鉛/ レギュラーガソリン	mu-en/regyurah-gasorin
up	上	ue
urgent	非常/緊急	hijoh/kinkyoo
urgently	早急に	sohkyoo-ni
urine	小便/おしっこ	shohben/oshikko
usually	たいてい	tigh-tay

V

vacate	立ち退く	tachi-noku
vaccinate	予防接種	yoboh sesshu

vagina	膣	*chitsu*
valid	価値のある	*kachi-no aru*
valley	谷	*tani*
valuable	高価な	*kohka-na*
van	中型ヴァン／ミニバス	*choogata-van/minibas*
vanilla	バニラ	*banira*
vase	花瓶	*kabin*
vaseline	ワセリン	*waserin*
veal	小牛の肉	*ko-ushi-no niku*
vegetable soup	野菜スープ	*ya-sigh soop*
vegetables	野菜	*ya-sigh*
vegetarian	ベジタリアン／菜食家	*bejitarian/sigh-shokka*
vein	静脈	*joh-myaku*
vending machine	自動販売機	*jidoh ham-bigh-ki*
venereal disease	性病	*say-byoh*
via	経由	*kay-yoo*
video camera	ビデオ・カメラ	*bideo-kamera*
video recorder	ビデオレコーダー	*bideo-rekohdah*
video tape	ビデオテープ	*bideo-tehpu*
view	眺め	*nagamay*
village	村	*mura*
visa	ビザ	*biza*
visit	訪問する	*hohmon suru*
visiting card	名刺	*mayshi*
visiting time	面会時間	*menkigh jikan*
vitamin tablets	ビタミン剤	*bitamin-zigh*
vitamins	ビタミン	*bitamin*
volcano	火山	*kazan*
volleyball	バレーボール	*baray-bohru*
vomit	吐く／戻す	*haku/modosu*

W

wait	待つ	*matsu*
waiter	ウェーター	*waytah*
waiting room	待合室	*machi-a-i-shitsu*
waitress	ウェイトレス	*waytresu*
wake up	起きる	*okiru*
Wales	ウェールズ	*wayruzu*
walk (noun)	散歩	*sampo*
walk (verb)	散歩する／歩く	*sampo suru/aruku*
wallet	財布	*sighfu*
warm	温かい	*atatakigh*
warn	注意する	*choo-i suru*
warning	注意	*choo-i*
wash	洗う	*ara-u*
washing	洗濯物	*sentaku-mono*
washing line	物干しロープ	*mono-hoshi rohp*
washing machine	洗濯機	*sentakki*
washing-powder	洗剤	*sen-zigh*
wasp	スズメバチ	*suzume-bachi*
watch	腕時計	*uday-do-kay*
water	水	*mizu*
water ski	水上スキーをする	*sweejoh skee-o suru*
watermill	水車	*sweesha*
waterproof	防水	*bohswee*
wave-pool	人工波プール／波のあるプール	*jinkoh-ha pooru/nami-no aru pooru*

way (direction)	方面	*hohmen*
way (method)	手段／方法	*shudan/hoh-hoh*
we	私達	*watash-tachi*
weak	弱い	*yowa-i*
weather	天気	*tenki*
weather forecast	天気予報	*tenki yo-hoh*
wedding	結婚式	*kekkon-shki*
Wednesday	水曜日	*swee-yoh-bi*
week	週	*shoo*
weekend	週末	*shoo-mats*
weekly ticket	一週間の定期券	*isshookan-no tayki-ken*
welcome	いらっしゃい	*irassha-i*
well (good)	いい／良い	*ee/yoi*
well (water)	井戸	*ido*
west	西	*nishi*
wet	濡れた	*nureta*
wetsuit	ウェット・スーツ	*wetto-soots*
what?	何	*nani*
wheel	車輪	*sharin*
wheelchair	車いす	*kuruma-isu*
when?	いつ	*itsu*
where?	どこ	*doko*
which?	どちら	*dochira*
whipped cream	ホイップクリーム	*hoippu-kreem*
white	白い	*shiro-i*
who?	誰	*daray*
why?	なぜ	*nazay*
wide-angle lens	広角レンズ	*kohkaku renzu*
widow	未亡人	*mibohjin*
widower	男やもめ	*otoko-yamomay*
wife (other's)	奥さま	*okusama*
wife (own)	妻	*tsuma*
wind	風	*kazay*
windbreak	風よけ	*kazay-yokay*
windmill	風車	*foosha*
window	窓	*mado*
window (of ticket office)	窓口	*mado-guchi*
windscreen wiper	ワイパー	*wigh-pah*
wine	ワイン	*wign*
wine card	ワインのメニュー	*wign-no menyoo*
wine shop	酒屋	*saka-ya*
winter	冬	*fuyu*
witness	証人	*shoh-nin*
woman	女	*onna*
wonderful (taste)	おいしい	*oy-shee*
wood	木	*ki*
wool (for knitting)	毛糸	*kay-to*
word	言葉	*kotoba*
work	仕事	*shi-goto*
working day (weekday)	平日	*hay-jits*
worn	古くなった	*furuku-natta*
worried	心配な	*shimpigh-na*
wound	傷	*kizu*
wrap	包む	*tsutsumu*
wrist	手首	*tekubi*
write	書く	*kaku*

write down	書く	*kaku*
writing pad	便箋	*binsen*
writing paper	便箋	*binsen*
wrong	間違った	*machi-gatta*

Y

yacht	ヨット	*yotto*
year	年	*toshi/nen*
yellow	黄色い	*kee-roy*
yes	はい	*high*
yes, please	はい、いただきます／	*high, itadaki-mas/*
	お願いします	*onegigh-shimas*
yesterday	昨日	*kinoh*
yoghurt	ヨーグルト	*yohguruto*
you	あなた	*anata*
you too	あなたも	*anata-mo*
youth hostel	ユースホステル	*yoos-hosteru*

Z

| zip | ファスナー／ジッパー | *fasunah/jippah* |
| zoo | 動物園 | *doh-butsu-en* |

Basic grammar

1 Sentence construction

The greatest difference between Japanese and English sentences is the position of the verb. In Japanese the verb always comes last, giving the basic structure as subject-object-verb:

sensei wa *michi* o **oshiemashita**   The teacher **showed** me the *way*

2 Parts of speech

Nouns Japanese nouns have no articles and no plural forms. **Zasshi** (magazine), for example, could mean a/the magazine, magazines, or the/some magazines. This might sound potentially confusing to English speakers who expect the clear distinctions that articles and plurals give. In actuality, though, very little confusion exists, because Japanese has ways of indicating number when it is necessary (see chapter 1).

Pronouns Japanese uses pronouns far less than English. They are in fact often omitted when in the subject position. In English we have to say <u>who</u> went in the sentence 'I went to Kyoto yesterday'; if it is clear you are talking about yourself, in Japanese you can merely say **'kinoo Kyoto e ikimashita'** (yesterday to-Kyoto went). The most frequently used pronouns in Japanese are **watashi** (I) and **anata** (you); 'he', 'she' and 'they' are far more uncommon.

Adjectives Like English, Japanese can use adjectives in two ways, before the noun they describe (**mushiatsui** hi, a **humid** day) or following it (kyoo wa **mushiatsui** desu, today is **humid**). In grammatical terms, adjectives can in fact function as verbs, and have tenses like verbs (see below).

Verbs The verb is probably the most important element in the Japanese sentence, since it is quite possible for the sentence to consist of a verb and nothing else:

tabemashita   (I, we, he, she, they, you, etc.) **ate**

Functions like tense, negation and level of politeness are shown by adding suffixes to the base form of the verb.

Whereas in English tense and agreement are probably the most important things about a verb, in Japanese the verb is the main way gradations of social status are marked. In the modern language there are three basic levels of politeness: the plain, or informal; the polite, or formal; and the honorific. If you look up a verb in the word list you will find it written in the base, or plain, form: for example, **taberu** (to eat) or **miru** (to see). This is the form used in informal conversation, so, for example, you might say to a friend 'ashita ii restoran ni **iku**' (tomorrow I'm going to a good restaurant). However, when you talk to people you have only just met or to someone senior to you, you must use the polite form, for example, 'ashita ii restoran ni **ikimasu**'. The **-masu** ending always indicates the polite level.

The honorific level is used when someone wishes to show extreme politeness, either because of their own humble position (a shop assistant to a customer, for example) or because of the exalted nature of the person he or she is speaking with (like a company president). Honorific language is very complicated and even Japanese people find it difficult. In the phrasebook, the informal level has been used in close personal situations, the polite in general conversation, and the honorific only when showing how someone in a service situation might address you.

In comparison with English the form of Japanese tenses is simple. The future tense has the same form as the present, so that **tabemasu** could mean 'I eat' or 'I will eat'. The past is shown by adding the suffix **ta**: tabemashi**ta** (I ate), mimashita (I saw). The only other form used for tense is the continuative, made using the suffix **te**: tabe**te** imasu (I am eating); tabe**te** imashita (I was eating). English speakers may find the lack of a perfect tense (I have done) confusing, but Japanese employs other, non-verb forms, to express this.

The negative is made by adding the suffix **nai** to the plain form of the verb, for example, tabe**nai** (I do not eat), or the suffix **n** to the polite **masu** ending, for example, tabemase**n** (I do not eat).

3 Particles

Japanese is very different from English in that the relationships between the various parts of speech are shown by the use of particles. English uses word order to indicate meaning: 'the dog bit the man' and 'the man bit the dog' are different entirely because of the order in which the words come in a sentence. In Japanese the meaning is not dependent on word order but on particles; the doer of the action (subject) is shown by the particle **ga** and receiver of the action (object) is shown by the particle **o**:

inu **ga** hito **o** kanda (literally, the dog-the man-bit: the dog bit the man)
inu **o** hito **ga** kanda (literally, the dog-the man-bit: the man bit the dog)

Japanese has another particle, **wa**, which often marks the subject as well. This has the function of pointing out a particular word and making it stand out from the rest of the sentence as the topic.

kono seki **wa** aite imasu ka? (as for this seat, is it free: is this seat free?)

koko ni **wa** nani ka omoshiroi no ga arimasu ka? (as for in this place, is there anything interesting here: is there anything interesting here?)

The above examples also show the use of the question-making particle **ka**.

Another important particle is **no**, used principally to join nouns together, so functioning like the English possessive.

watashi **no** namae (literally, the name of me; my name)
igirisu **no** shimbun (literally, a newspaper of England; an English newspaper)

Other particles act like English prepositions: **ni** (at, in, on, to), **e** (to a place), **de** (at, with), **kara** (from), **made** (to, until), and **yori** (from).

4 Some useful grammatical forms

The phrase book has shown you how to say things as you need them in different situations. Let us bring together some useful forms that might help you to make new sentences, using words from the wordlist.

Please do something A general imperative is the **-te kudasai (-te kuda-sigh)** ending added to a verb:

taberu (eat)	tabe**te kudasai**	please eat
miseru (show)	mise**te kudasai**	please show me
kuru (come)	ki**te kudasai**	please come
kaku (write)	kai**te kudasai**	please write

You can negate this with the phrase **naide kudasai (nigh-de kuda-sigh)**:

taberu	tabe**naide kudasai**	please don't eat
miseru	mise**naide kudasai**	please don't show me
kuru	ko**naide kudasai**	please don't come
kaku	kaka**naide kudasai**	please don't write

Have to do The most usual way of showing necessity is **-nakereba narimasen**:

iku	ika**nakereba narimasen**	I have to go
suru	shi**nakereba narimasen**	I have to do
miru	mi**nakereba narimasen**	I have to see

Want You can show that you want to do something by adding **-tai n(o) desu (-tigh n(o) des)** to the verb:

iku	iki**tai n desu**	I want to go
yomu	yomi**tai n desu**	I want to read
miru	mi**tai n desu**	I want to see

Please When you want someone to do something for you, say **onegai shimasu**, literally 'I beg of you'. This is a useful phrase that can be used in a variety of ways. If someone offers to do something for you, you can use it to accept:

biiru wa doo desu ka	would you like some beer?
Onegai shimasu	yes, please

If you want an item in a shop, say what it is with **onegai shimasu**:

hon onegai shimasu	a book, please
pan onegai shimasu	bread, please

Useful verbs Two of the most useful verbs are **desu (des)**, equivalent of is/are and **arimasu (arimas)**, 'there is/are':

watashi wa Igirisujin **desu**	I **am** English
aita heya wa **arimasu ka**	**are there** any vacancies?

5 A final tip

The Japanese language is full of loan words, most of them from English. They are used to name things, and so are almost always nouns. If you get stuck for a word, try pronouncing the English word slowly in a Japanese way. For example, if you pronounce 'bus station' syllable by syllable, *ba-su su-tay-shon*, this will turn out to be a perfectly understandable Japanese word.

The Japanese writing system

Written Japanese combines three different scripts, *hiragana, katakana* and *kanji. Hiragana* consists of 46 syllabic characters and is used to write the grammatical elements of the Japanese sentence, like particles and verb endings. *Katakana* also has 46 characters, and is used to write foreign words. The meaningful component of the sentence is written with *kanji* (Chinese characters), that is, nouns, adjectives, some adverbs and the base form of verbs.

Igirisu no **hon** o **ka**imashita   I bought an English book

Igirisu will be written in *katakana*, being a foreign word, **hon** and **ka** in Chinese characters, and the remaining syllables in *hiragana*.

Place names on station notice boards will almost always be written in *kanji*, but the pronunciation in *hiragana* is also given beneath. In the large cities, the pronunciation in the Latin alphabet (*romaji*, 'Roman letters') will also appear. The *kanji* give the meaning to the word. For example, To-kyo means 'eastern capital', O-saka means 'great slope', Hane-da means 'field of wings' and Roppon-gi means 'six trees'.